INVITATION
TO THE
NEW TESTAMENT

A Short-Term **DISCIPLE** Bible Study

INVITATION TO THE NEW TESTAMENT

PARTICIPANT BOOK

David deSilva
& Emerson Powery

Abingdon Press
Nashville

A Short-term DISCIPLE Bible Study

INVITATION TO THE NEW TESTAMENT

Copyright © 2005 by Abingdon Press

Scripture quotations, unless otherwise indicated, are from the NEW REVISED STANDARD VERSION OF THE BIBLE. Copyright © 1989 by the Division of Christian Education of the National Council of the Churches of Christ in the USA. Used by permission. All rights reserved.

Cover photo credit: *The Last Supper, Jesus and His Disciples* (Mosaic). S. Apollinare Nuove, Ravenna, Italy. Erich Lessing / Art Resource, NY.

Development Staff: Mark Price, Senior Editor; Cindy Caldwell, Development Editor; Leo Ferguson, Designer.

06 07 08 09 10 11 12 13 14 — 10 9 8 7 6 5
MANUFACTURED IN THE UNITED STATES OF AMERICA

Contents

Meet the Writers

DAVID A. DESILVA is Trustees' Professor of New Testament and Greek at Ashland Theological Seminary in Ashland, Ohio, and an elder in the Florida Annual Conference of The United Methodist Church. David has been a video presenter in previous DISCIPLE Bible studies and is author of *An Introduction to the New Testament, Introducing the Apocrypha, Praying with John Wesley,* and commentaries on Hebrews and Fourth Maccabees. He lives with his wife and three sons in Ashland, Ohio, where he is also Director of Music at Christ United Methodist Church.

EMERSON B. POWERY is Chair of the Department of Theology and Associate Professor of New Testament and Christian Origins at Lee University in Cleveland, Tennessee. Emerson is host for the revised DISCIPLE: BECOMING DISCIPLES THROUGH BIBLE STUDY videos and co-editor of the forthcoming *African American New Testament Commentary.* Emerson and his wife, Kimberly, have four sons, Matthew Byron, Jason Alexander, Samuel Emerson, and Preston James. When Emerson is not teaching hermenetics or researching some minute exegetical point on the Gospels, he loves to play racquetball (with his colleagues), play chess (with his sons), and visit used book stores (with Kimberly).

An Invitation to this Study

The study you are about to begin is one in a series of short-term, in-depth, small group Bible studies based on the design of DISCIPLE Bible Study. Like the series of long-term DISCIPLE studies, this study has been developed with these underlying assumptions:

- the Bible is the primary text of study
- preparation on the part of participants is expected
- the study leader acts as a facilitator rather than as a lecturer
- a weekly group session features small group discussion
- video presentations by scholars set the Scriptures in context
- encouraging and enhancing Christian discipleship is the goal of study

This participant book is your guide to the study and preparation you will do prior to the weekly group meeting. To establish a disciplined pattern of study, first choose a time and a place where you can read, take notes, reflect, and pray. Then choose a good study Bible.

CHOOSING AND USING A STUDY BIBLE

Again, keep in mind the Bible is *the* text for all short-term DISCIPLE Bible studies, not the participant book; the function of the participant book is to help persons read and listen to the Bible. So because the Bible is the key to this study, consider a couple of recommendations in choosing a good study version of the Bible.

First: The Translation

The recommended translation is the New Revised Standard Version (NRSV). It is recommended for two reasons: (1) It is a reliable, accurate translation, and (2) it is used in the preparation of all DISCIPLE study manuals.

However, any reliable translation can be used. In fact, having available several different translations is a good practice. Some of them include the NIV, NJB, REB, RSV, NKJV, NAB. To compare the many English translations of the Bible before choosing, consider consulting the book *Choosing a Bible: A Guide to Modern English Translations and Editions* by Steven Sheeley and Robert Nash, Jr.

Keep in mind that the *Living Bible* and *The Message*, while popular versions of the Bible, are not considered translations. They are paraphrases.

Second: The Study Features

The recommended Bible to use in any study is, of course, a study Bible, that is, a Bible containing notes, introductions to each book, charts, maps, and other helps designed to deepen and enrich the study of the biblical text. Because there are so many study Bibles available today, be sure to choose one based on some basic criteria:

- The introductory articles to each book or groups of books are helpful to you in summarizing the main features of those books.

- The notes *illuminate* the text of Scripture by defining words, making cross-references to similar passages, and providing cultural or historical background. Keep in mind that mere volume of notes is not necessarily an indication of their value.

- The maps, charts and other illustrations display important biblical/historical data in a form that is accurate and accessible.

- Any glossaries, dictionaries, concordances or indexes in the Bible are easily located and understood.

All study Bibles attempt, in greater or lesser degree, to strike a balance between *interpreting* for the reader what the text means and *helping* the reader understand what the text says. Study Bible notes are conveyed through the interpretive lens of those who prepare the notes. Regardless of what study Bible you choose to use, though, always be mindful of which part of the page is Scripture and which part is not.

GETTING THE MOST FROM READING THE BIBLE

Read the Bible with curiosity. Ask the questions, *who? what? where? when? how?* and *why?* as you read.

Learn as much as you can about the passage you are studying. Try to discover what the writer was saying for the time in which the passage was written. Be familiar with the surrounding verses and chapters to establish a passage's setting or situation.

Pay attention to the form of a passage of Scripture. How you read and understand poetry or parable will differ from how you read and understand historical narrative.

Above all, let Scripture speak for itself, even if the apparent meaning is troubling or unclear. Question Scripture, but also seek answers to your questions in Scripture itself. Often the biblical text will solve some of the problems that arise in certain passages. Consult additional reference resources when needed. And remember to trust the Holy Spirit to guide you in your study.

MAKING USE OF ADDITIONAL RESOURCES

Though you will need only the Bible and this participant book to have a meaningful experience, these basic reference books may help you go deeper in to your study of Scripture.

- *Eerdmans Dictionary of the Bible*, edited by David Noel Freedman (William B. Eerdmans, Grand Rapids, 2000).

- *Dictionary of New Testament Background*, edited by Craig A. Evans and Stanley E. Porter (InterVarsity Press, Downers Grove, IL, 2000).

- *Eerdmans Commentary on the Bible*, edited by James D. G. Dunn and John W. Rogerson (William B. Eerdmans, Grand Rapids, 2003).

- *An Introduction to the New Testament: Contexts, Methods, and Ministry Formation,* by David A. deSilva (InterVarsity Press, Downers Grove, IL, 2004).

- *The New Interpreter's Bible: A Commentary in Twelve Volumes,* (Abingdon Press, Nashville, 1995–2002)

MAKING USE OF THE PARTICIPANT BOOK

The participant book serves two purposes. First, it is your study guide: use it to structure your daily reading of the assigned Scripture passages, and to prompt your reflection on what you read. Second, it is your note-taking journal: use it to write down any insights, comments, and questions you want to recall and perhaps make use of in your group's discussions.

As you will see, the daily reading assignments for each session call for reading the Scripture passages *before* reading the commentary by the study writers. This is intentional. The commentary is full of references to the assigned readings from the Bible and was prepared by writers who assumed that their readers would be knowledgeable of the week's Scriptures before coming to the commentary. So the recommended approach to this study is to let the biblical writers have their say first.

Introduction

Jesus stood at the center of the early church's understanding of itself and of the movement of God into church members' lives. Early Christians may have entertained a great deal of diversity regarding the significance of the person of Jesus and the implications of following this Jesus, but they could agree that Jesus was definitive for their experience of, and response to, God. The reader of the New Testament quickly discovers this to be true as well for the early Christian leaders who left us this rich legacy of sacred texts. Jesus reveals the character and purposes of God. Jesus becomes the focal lens through which Christians understand and connect with their Jewish heritage. Jesus provides the model for living in line with God's purposes, especially when that means overstepping deeply entrenched boundaries between people, persevering in the face of hostility, or embodying a new set of values that elevates servanthood above self-promotion. Looking to Jesus, Christian disciples locate themselves in sacred time, looking back upon his death and resurrection and forward to his coming again, as the compass points by which they must navigate their course through this life.

This invitation to the New Testament therefore takes the story of Jesus—the story that is paradigmatic for the church's own identity, mission, and theology—as its starting point. In particular, this invitation to explore the New Testament begins with the Gospel according to Matthew as the starting point for each session. Matthew's portrait of Jesus was chosen not simply because this Gospel opens the New Testament. Rather, Matthew's Gospel was chosen because of its intentional arrangement as a resource for understanding Jesus' teachings and applying them to life together as the church. Early Christian leaders recognized this and consistently turned to Matthew as the choice for catechesis, the instruction of new converts in the way of discipleship. From this starting point, participants are then invited into dialogue with the ways other New Testament writers wrestled with the issues and implications of the story of Jesus for the formation of disciples and communities of faith, working out his story in their own stories.

Why call this study an invitation to the New Testament? First, it is an invitation simply to read portions of the New Testament itself. Readings for the first five days of each week invite you to immerse yourself in Matthew's Gospel and in other texts that are thematically related to the issues raised in Matthew.

Second, it is an invitation to conversation *about* the New Testament, especially about how to understand the various texts "in context," on their *own* terms, rather than on *our* terms. The reading for the sixth day (the "commentary") begins this process, which is further supplemented by the video segments presented in the class session. The model of "conversation" has been woven in throughout this process of writing and developing this study. Not only were we in constant conversation with one another throughout the process, but we also divided the tasks of writing the commentary material for the participant book and the video commentary in such a way as to enhance this sense of dialogue. For example, the Part 1 video segment for each session features the commentator who did *not* take the lead in writing the participant's guide for that session, so that the participants can hear a second voice each week. The Part 2 video segment invites the participant into a conversation with the writers of the study and a guest scholar who will bring yet another perspective on the issues raised by the texts.

Finally, this study will serve as an invitation to ongoing study of the Bible, both Old and New Testaments. For it is, finally, in conversation with these sacred texts that we discover anew our identity in God, our community with one another, and our calling to serve God's vision for the world.

Jesus Calls Us into God's Redemption Story

INTRODUCTION

Who do you say that I am?" Since Jesus first confronted his disciples with this question (Matt 16:15), the way we answer the question has direct consequences for how we will relate to God and respond to the invitation to new life found in the New Testament. In this week's readings, we explore anew why early Christians called Jesus the "Son of Abraham," "Son of David," and "Son of God," and what such faith statements tell us about how encountering Jesus involves us in God's larger work of redeeming a people for God.

DAILY ASSIGNMENTS

As you read this week's assignments, observe carefully (1) what claims are being made about Jesus' identity, (2) what significance these claims are said to have for us in terms of our connection with God, and (3) what responses are reflected or promoted in each text as people encounter this Jesus.

DAY ONE: Matthew 1–4

Throughout Matthew we find a special interest in developing connections between Jesus' life and teaching and the revelation of God in the Hebrew Scriptures. Pay attention to the ways in which Matthew roots Jesus in the story of God's people, Israel, and the specific connections he makes with that story.

DAY TWO: Luke 1–4

The opening of Luke reads like many passages about God's redemptive activity in the Old Testament, even as it redirects the hope of the Old Testament away from the "Jewish nation" to a more inclusive "people of God." Pay special attention to the statements about how God's promises find their fruition in Jesus, and how the early Christians' understanding of those promises is being transformed.

DAY THREE: Acts 2:22-39; 3:13-26; Galatians 3

These three passages examine the significance of Jesus within the larger plan of God from several different angles. Note carefully again how Jesus connects with God's long-standing plans and promises, and what God makes available to people in Jesus.

DAY FOUR: John 1; Hebrews 1–2

Today's readings make some of the loftiest claims about Jesus to be found anywhere in the New Testament. Reflect as you read on what these texts have to say about the relationship between encountering Jesus and knowing God.

DAY FIVE: John 6:22-71; Acts 9:1-31

These two stories bring into sharp focus the strong reactions people have as they encounter Jesus and claims made regarding Jesus' identity and significance. As you read, observe what factors contribute to making an encounter with Jesus positively life-changing, and what factors contribute to rejection of Jesus.

DAY SIX: Read the commentary in the participant book.

PUTTING DOWN ROOTS

Tracing a family tree is a strange beginning for a book by modern standards, hardly an attention-grabber. But for Matthew and his first readers, a genealogy was an important statement about a person's significance. It located a person in a particular family with a particular story and thereby located a person in the world. Where we might start by highlighting individual achievement, "identity" for Matthew starts with a person's community and ancestry.

The first thing Matthew wants to say about Jesus is that he is deeply rooted in the story of Israel and, indeed, is the natural outworking and culmination of that story. Israel's story is a story about God's promises to bring peace and wholeness to humankind through God's chosen means. God promised Abraham a sea of descendants, through whom all nations would be blessed: "I will bless those who bless you ... and in you all the families of the earth shall be blessed" (Gen 12:3; see also Gen 22:18). Similarly, God promised David a descendant whose throne God would "establish forever" and with whom God would relate as Father to child: "I will be a father to him, and he shall be a son to me" (2 Sam 7:14; see also Ps 2:7). Matthew shows from the opening paragraph how Jesus, as descendant of Abraham and David, is an appropriate person through whom God's promises to Abraham and David would find their fulfillment and their stories find a climax.

> **Israel's story is a story about God's promises to bring peace and wholeness to humankind through God's chosen means.**

Matthew's genealogy is not just a list of names. It is a theological statement about Jesus. He arranges this genealogy so that there are exactly fourteen generations between the significant points in Israel's story: God's selection of Abraham as the vehicle for blessing; God's selection of David as the vehicle for God's rule; the apparent collapse of the promises in the destruction of Jerusalem and the Exile; the birth of Jesus, in whom all God's promises are renewed and Israel's fortunes restored (Matt 1:17-18). By doing so, Matthew subtly hints that God's divine plan is thus working itself out in a measured and orderly way, leading through the history of Israel to the coming of Jesus. It is all the more apparent that Matthew's genealogy is crafted to make certain points rather than simply supply a list of ancestors as with Luke's genealogy (Luke 3:23-38).

16

Both the Matthean and Lucan genealogies, however, push beyond the traditional lines within community. Matthew includes four women, three of whom (Rahab, Ruth, and "the wife of Uriah") are non-Jews and three of whom (Tamar, Rahab, and Ruth) highlight "anomalous" conceptions in some way, underscoring the place of both women and Gentiles in the community of God. Luke presses further, tracing Jesus' genealogy past Abraham all the way back to Adam and to God. Since Abraham is known primarily as the ancestor of the Jewish nation, tracing Jesus' lineage back to Adam and to God brings out the universal scope of God's action on behalf of humanity both in creation and in the sending of Jesus not only for the benefit of the Jewish people but also for the benefit of all people, bringing together into one body the one humanity God originally created us to be.

> **DIG DEEPER**
>
> Learn more about the four women in Matthew's genealogy:
>
> • Tamar (Gen. 38:11-30)
> • Rahab (Josh 2; 6:22-25)
> • Ruth (Book of Ruth)
> • Bathsheba (2 Sam 11; 12:24)
>
> What qualities do they add to Jesus' human heritage? What does their inclusion in Jesus' family tree teach about God's purposes?

GOD REMEMBERS GOD'S PROMISES

Luke's story of the annunciation and birth of Jesus resonates deeply with Matthew's desire to connect Jesus with Abraham and David. The angel's announcement and the songs of Mary and Zechariah all proclaim that, in Jesus' birth, God "makes good" on the promises God gave to Abraham and David (Luke 1:32-33, 54-55, 68-73). Jesus' coming is the fruit of God "remembering" God's mercy to help Israel and "remembering" God's covenant with Israel (Luke 1:54, 72). The point is that the first place to look for clues about Jesus' significance is to the faith and hope of Israel.

Paul also does this to an extraordinary degree. Even while he is arguing that following Jesus means that the Jewish law is no longer the binding rule on the community, he anchors faith in Jesus in God's promise to Abraham. Looking closely at the actual wording of the promise, Paul notices that the text of Genesis 12:7 and 22:17-18 actually says that the promise is given to Abraham "and to his seed" (Gal 3:16). Of course, "seed" might more naturally refer to all Abraham's offspring; but Paul uses a familiar Jewish technique of biblical interpretation—looking at the literal sense of the Scripture. Paul therefore identifies Jesus as the "seed" of Abraham through whom the promised blessing would come to all the nations, namely that "we might receive the promise of the Spirit through faith" (Gal 3:14).

Another way that New Testament writers root Jesus in the distinctive hope and theology of the Hebrew Scriptures is by seeing the details of his life and the lives of those around him (like John the Baptizer) reflected in the prophecies and psalms of the Old Testament. This is the role of what are called the "prophecy and fulfillment" formulas in Matthew 1:22-23; 2:6, 15, 18; 3:15-16: "All this took place to fulfill what had been spoken by the Lord through the prophet...." By means of these side comments, Matthew invites us to see some facet of Old Testament promise becoming reality in the life of Jesus. On one hand, we could criticize Matthew for not reading those Old Testament texts in the context of early Israelite history. On the other hand, we could appreciate the way Matthew sees the whole history of Israel from its Exodus (Matt 2:15) to its Exile (Matt 2:18) to its hope for renewal (Matt 1:22-23; 2:6; 3:15-16) taking on flesh and fulfillment in the life of Jesus.

SON OF DAVID, SON OF GOD

In his most mature statement of his gospel, Paul speaks of Jesus as "Son of David," in terms of his human lineage, and "Son of God," by virtue of his resurrection (Rom 1:3-4). Both of these titles are closely related in the New Testament since the royal ideology of ancient Israel depicted the Davidic monarch as God's Son. When God promises David a descendant to rule after him, God says: "I will be a father to him, and he shall be a son to me" (2 Sam 7:14). Likewise, at religious festivals celebrating the enthronement of the Davidic king, singers would intone the words of Psalm 2 on behalf of the king: "I will tell of the decree of the LORD: He said to me: 'You are my son; today I have begotten you'" (Ps 2:7).

This background helps us see that it was not so far a leap for early Christians to talk about Jesus' relationship to God in terms of Father and Son (as in Hebrews 1:1-6; Acts 2:34-35, which explicitly quote the royal psalms and other psalms connected with David), once they identified him as the promised heir to the throne of David. The fact that God would "give to him the throne of his ancestor David" naturally meant that he would also "be called the Son of the Most High" (Luke 1:32). Here, as in Paul's understanding of Abraham's singular "seed," Jesus is also understood not as one heir among many, but *the* heir to David's throne and as God's Son. The narratives that identify the Holy Spirit as the begetter of Jesus (Matt 1:18, 20; Luke 1:35) also give clear witness to the conviction of the early church: Jesus is God's Son and, as heir of David, epitomizes how God provides leadership for God's people. As Matthew will make clear, this is the leadership of a servant, a redeemer who gives his life for the deliverance of his people.

The New Testament writers do not stop with traditions about David and his heir, however. They also look to Jewish traditions about "Wisdom" to talk about who Jesus is. Wisdom is a rather abstract idea about the divine ordering of the cosmos and about how we must perceive that order to live intelligently. Jewish writers, however, began to personify Wisdom, presenting her as a female spirit-being who stood as mediator between God and creation, and between God and humanity, connecting people to God as they walked in accordance with Wisdom. She was created at the very beginning of God's creative activity (Prov 8:22) and worked alongside God in the creation of heaven and earth and in the ongoing maintenance of the world (Prov 8:27-31; Wis 8:1; 9:9). The Wisdom of Solomon, a Jewish text from the turn of the era found in the Apocrypha, goes even further, depicting Wisdom as "a pure emanation of the glory of the Almighty ... a reflection of eternal light ... and an image of his goodness" (Wis 7:25-26), who enters human souls and "makes them friends of God" (Wis 7:27).

> **The New Testament writers root Jesus in the distinctive hope and theology of the Hebrew Scriptures by seeing the details of his life and the lives of those around him (like John the Baptizer) reflected in the prophecies and psalms of the Old Testament.**

The clear stamp of these traditions can be seen in the attributes of the "Son" as "the reflection of God's glory and the exact imprint of God's very being" in Hebrews 1:2-3, as "image of the invisible God" in Colossians 1:15-17, and in the activity of the Word in creation in John 1:1-18. Early Christians discovered the new face of Wisdom in the face of Jesus. In Jesus we see how God interacts with creation in life-giving, life-sustaining, order-creating ways. John goes even further. Because the Son is the clear reflection of the Father, just as Wisdom was the "shine" (better than "reflection") produced by God's "light," Jesus is the "exegesis"—the studied explanation and "unpacking"—of the very character of God (John 1:18).

To see him is to see the unseen God and thus to come to understand the holiness of God in terms of the love, mercy, and restorative compassion shown and taught by Jesus.

WHERE THIS STORY IS HEADING

The language about Jesus as the Son of God does not emphasize the distance between Jesus and us. Rather, this title shows how fully Jesus as God's Son became human and entered flesh so as to bring us close to himself and to God: "since ... the children share flesh and blood, he himself likewise shared the same things" (Heb 2:14; see also 2:10-18). Both Matthew and Luke underscore Jesus' identity as "Son of God" not just in the birth stories, but also in the stories of Jesus' baptism and temptation. In the stories of his baptism, Jesus identifies himself so closely with humanity's need to respond to God with repentant heart that he is declared by God's own voice to be "my Son, the Beloved" (Matt 3:17; Luke 3:22). As Son of God, Jesus shows us that our journey back to God begins in the waters of baptism and in the change of heart and life that this signifies. In the accounts of his temptation, Satan tests Jesus' identity as "God's Son" (Matt 4:3, 6; Luke 4:3, 9) and what it means to act as God's Son in the world. Here we find a window into how Jesus learned to be a "sympathetic high priest" who knows what it means to be tested by life's trials and enticements, so we can rely on him for the help we need, following him as the children of God (Heb 2:17-18; see also 4:14-15). It is also here that we see how Jesus entered into single combat with Satan on our behalf to "free those who all their lives were held in slavery by the fear of death" (Heb 2:15). This combat was not complete until Jesus embraced death in obedience to God, winning the struggle that all of the many sons and daughters would face as they, too, would be assailed by both threats and enticements to give up the pursuit of life with God.

Jesus' identity as "Son of God" is ultimately, then, about his opening up of a way for us to be reborn as "children of God," to be saved from our sins (Matt 1:21), and to live a life "with God" made possible by "Emmanuel... God is with us" (Matt 1:23). We see the first steps of that path here in the renunciation of the self-serving life of sin through baptism and through the ongoing contest against the Enemy of our souls. As the story unfolds, we will see in Jesus' teachings an example of what it means to follow *this* Son to glory.

INVITATION TO DISCIPLESHIP

When people encounter Jesus and are confronted with the claims concerning his identity and significance, they can respond in several different ways. How we respond is of decisive importance.

Confronted with Jesus' own claim to embody the work of the Servant of God described by Isaiah (Isa 61:1-2; Luke 4:18-21) and with Jesus' explanation that this Servant comes not to serve the national and ethnic interests of Judeans but the renewal of all people (observed in Luke 4:25-27 and in the inclusiveness of Matthew's genealogy), Jesus' own townspeople respond with violent rejection. Do we have room in our lives for a Jesus who challenges our dearly held boundaries and invites us into a larger vision for the community of faith?

Confronted by their neighbors' hostile response to their faith in Jesus, and by marginalization in society, some of the Christians addressed by the Letter to the Hebrews begin to seek a way back into their former, comfortable lives. By "neglecting to meet together" (Heb 10:24-25), they also stand in danger of neglecting the Word God speaks to them in the Son (Heb 2:1-4) and are challenged to keep responding fully and appropriately to the Son's invitation. Do we place the priority on responding to Jesus' invitation in a way appropriate to his value as the Son of God, or do our priorities show a dangerous neglect of his word?

Confronted with the need to repent and return to God (Matt 3:1-10; Luke 3:1-14; Acts 2:37-39; 3:19-21), to change the entire direction of their lives (Acts 9), many allow themselves to be "cut to the heart" and begin again. Do we have the humility before God to acknowledge the distance between our lives and God's desires and the courage to start in a new direction?

Challenged with Jesus' invitation to leave behind the trade, the village, and the life they knew so well, two sets of brothers set out into the unknown future of following wherever Jesus leads (Matt 4:18-22). Do we so understand the surpassing value of walking with Jesus that we, too, would rather journey with him than stay in our areas of comfort and familiarity? "I am the light of the world. Whoever follows me will never walk in darkness but will have the light of life" (John 8:12).

FOR REFLECTION

- How has Jesus challenged some of your "dearly held" boundaries?

- How does the way you respond to Jesus' claim on your life reflect your priorities?

- When have you acknowledged the need to return to God? What did it take to move in God's direction?

- How has Jesus enlarged your vision of what constitutes the community of faith?

Jesus Calls Us to a Transformed Life

INTRODUCTION

Following Jesus is not just about believing the right things concerning Jesus; it is also about living according to his example and teaching. Jesus, James, Paul, and other New Testament voices all emphasize this point: discipleship means the pursuit of a just and holy life that is fully pleasing to God. In this regard, they continue the invitation of Moses and the prophets to a transformed life but now with a special emphasis on the gift of the Holy Spirit, who guides the disciple in, and empowers the disciple for, living that transformed life.

DAILY ASSIGNMENTS

As you read this week's assigned Scripture texts, take special note of the ways that following Jesus should shape our everyday attitudes and behaviors. What are Jesus' expectations for his followers? What practical differences do Paul and James expect "calling Jesus 'Lord'" to make in the disciple's life? What roles do both "faith" and "works" play in our lives?

DAY ONE: Matthew 5–7

The Sermon on the Mount lays out a bold and challenging vision for a life that is "righteous" before God. Look for the reasons Jesus gives for embracing this vision and for what these ethical teachings tell us about God.

DAY TWO: James

In a manner reminiscent of the Sermon on the Mount at many points, James also describes behaviors that are in keeping with life in God and behaviors that are more in keeping with the untransformed life. Pay attention once again to the reasons that James gives for these ethical guidelines and what he has to say about integrity of belief and action.

DAY THREE: Romans 1–4

Paul speaks in broad strokes of God's expectations of humanity, human failure, and how God worked to overcome those failures and close the distance between God's righteousness and God's creatures. Note how Paul uses these themes to break down the barrier between Jews and Gentiles and establish a new, shared foundation for all people to respond to God's new initiatives in Christ.

DAY FOUR: Romans 6–8

Today's reading focuses on our response to God's revelation of right-eousness in Jesus and the "newness of life" into which God invites us. As you read, observe the connections Paul makes between what has happened to us through Jesus and the new direction and possibilities that open up as a result.

DAY FIVE: 1 Corinthians 5–6

We see Paul at work here dealing with the challenges of living as disciples amid real-life challenges, temptations, and tendencies. What impulses are disciples called to curb rather than indulge? What reasons are given for excluding these behaviors?

DAY SIX: Read the commentary in participant book.

"HEARING" IS NOT ENOUGH

One feature of Matthew's Gospel that helped it rise to prominence in the early church is that the evangelist collected so many sayings and teachings of Jesus (in distinction from Mark) *and* tried to arrange these in five meaningful, discrete blocks (outdoing Luke in this regard). This is often seen as an indication that Jesus' words provide the "New Pentateuch" (the Pentateuch is a name for the "five books of Moses" that contain the Law), the new rule of life, for the Christian community. Matthew provided a convenient and well-organized repository of Jesus' instruction, and therefore became the most used and useful Gospel for instructing new believers on what it meant to "follow" this Jesus.

> In the end, it is not the beliefs one professes, but the deeds one does that reveal the heart and have value before God.

The first of these five blocks of teaching is known as the "Sermon on the Mount." (The others are the commissioning speech in Matthew 10, the collection of parables of the Kingdom in Chapter 13, the "community rule" in Chapter 18, and the "end-time discourse" in Chapters 24–25). As Jesus' first public teaching in Matthew, the Sermon on the Mount is often regarded as a representative summary of Jesus' ethical philosophy. It is a collection of sayings that provides a series of "snapshots" of what truly righteous living looks like—that "righteousness" without which we "will never enter the kingdom of heaven" (Matt 5:20).

Jesus' teaching is so challenging, however, and his standards of righteousness so high that interpreters have had a very difficult time believing that Jesus really meant for his followers to live this way. Some have suggested that the real purpose of the Sermon on the Mount is to drive people to despair of ever being sufficiently righteous to gain entrance into God's kingdom, leading them therefore to abandon their "own righteousness" in favor of God's righteousness. This interpretation marks the triumph of Paul (as expressed in Rom 10:3-4) over Matthew. Or, perhaps more accurately, the triumph of Protestant theology and its fear of "works righteousness" over both Paul and Matthew, for whom good works are still essential marks of the genuine disciple! Others suggest that Jesus taught this radical way of living as an "interim ethic," meant for a supposedly brief period between Jesus' ministry and the Second Coming. But as the centuries yawned between those two events, living according to the teachings of the Sermon on the Mount became impractical.

Both suggestions tame the challenge of the Sermon on the Mount and render it comfortably irrelevant. Both also fail to grasp Jesus' own perspective that his "yoke," the instruction he lays upon his disciples, is truly "light" and "easy" (Matt 11:28-30). Here faith must exercise itself, faith that living by Jesus' teachings—"doing what he says"—will truly lead to a freer and less oppressive way of life than our natural inclinations or rationalized ethics provide. Here faith must exercise itself in another way as well, as faithfulness or loyalty to the One we name "Lord," a name that only has meaning insofar as we yield to Jesus' claim on our obedience and our commitment to live out his vision of righteousness.

Support for the conclusion that Jesus meant for his followers to live according to his teaching—even such challenging ethical ideals as we find in the Sermon on the Mount—is readily found as we see other early Christian leaders using the Sermon on the Mount as a resource for shaping Christian conduct. James, Jesus' brother and leader of the Jerusalem church, writes his Epistle from beginning to end as if Jesus' words should guide the disciples' attitudes and responses in a wide variety of situations. James echoes Jesus' claim that his followers must put into practice what they heard taught by him: "be doers of the word, and not merely hearers who deceive themselves" (Jas 1:22; see also Matt 7:24-27). In the end, it is not the beliefs one professes, but the deeds one does that reveal the heart and have value before God (see Jas 2:14; Matt 7:21).

THE CONTINUITY BETWEEN LAW AND GOSPEL

If Jesus' teachings are binding for his followers, what about the Law of Moses (the Torah), that core body of instruction that was binding for all Jews? The authority of the Torah in the early church was the focus of considerable debate during the first century of Christian discipleship, and a particularly pressing one. For Jewish Christians, this was a question of vital importance since the Torah had been the source of their identity and the covenant the basis for their relationship with God. But both Gentile and Jewish Christians accepted the Jewish Scriptures as divine revelation, and the Law of Moses occupied a prominent place in that body of revelation. It also occupies a prominent place in Jesus' teaching.

In fact, the Sermon on the Mount provides some of the best clues about how Jesus understood the relationship between the Law and his own teachings. Six times Jesus says, "You have heard that it was said to those of ancient times.... But I say to you ..." (Matt 5:21, 27, 31, 33, 38, 43). This particular literary device, called "antithesis," could give the impression that Jesus sets himself and his teaching radically against the Jewish law, but a closer look shows otherwise. In Matthew 5:21-30, Jesus actually deepens and extends the application of two of the Ten Commandments, teaching that the righteousness for which God calls extends to speech, attitude, and even how we perceive other people (e.g., not as obstacles with which to be angry or objects for our lust, both of which prevent our loving our neighbor as ourselves). Then in Matthew 5:31-42, Jesus removes the loopholes, as it were, from the law, concessions given to human beings that made room, in fact, for living with less than the righteousness that God desires. Finally in Matthew 5:43-48, Jesus transcends the limited interpretations placed on the command to love one's neighbor and calls his followers to reflect God's character in their own generosity and goodness toward both friend and enemy. In so doing, Jesus reaffirms the central premise of Leviticus—that we are to "be holy" as the Lord "is holy" (Lev 11:44-45; 19:2)—as binding on his followers but redefines how that "holiness" is to be understood and reflected (compare how Luke 6:36 and 1 Pet 1:14-16 also reinterpret this commandment from Leviticus). By following Jesus, its most authoritative interpreter, the disciple of Jesus does not abandon God's law, but rather learns how to fulfill it more perfectly. In this way, those who follow Jesus can claim to stand in continuity with the Torah, even when they do not live it out "according to the letter."

> **Jesus regarded the community of his followers as standing in continuity with the historic people of God and their ethical tradition, as a renewal rather than a replacement.**

The continuity between Jesus and the ethical life of the first covenant is also made apparent as Jesus affirms and incorporates the passion of the prophets for the poor and for justice in human relationships, as well as many lessons learned from the Jewish wisdom tradition and other ethical teachings within Judaism. Thus the instruction of Yeshua Ben Sira, a sage leading a school in Jerusalem around the end of the third century B.C., that people must forgive each other their offenses if they hoped to be forgiven by God, also becomes a distinctive emphasis of Jesus' teaching (compare Sir 28:2-4 with Matt 6:12, 14-15). Similarly, Jesus approves and incorporates the instruction that we should pray and do good for the one who wishes to harm us taught in the *Testament of Joseph* (18:2; see Matt 5:43-48). Such connections make it very clear that Jesus regarded the community of his followers as standing in continuity with the historic people of God and their ethical tradition, as a renewal rather than a replacement.

James similarly reaffirms the ongoing validity of the Torah as a revelation of the ethical standards that disciples must embody. He also holds up the prohibitions against murder and adultery and the command to love the neighbor as abiding statutes (Jas 2:8, 11), directing his readers to their accountability to the "law of liberty" (Jas 1:25; 2:12), the ethical heritage of Torah as interpreted and taught by Jesus. It might be surprising to some readers to discover that Paul also affirms the validity of the standards taught in the Torah. One stands judged or excused on the Day of Judgment insofar as one has manifested or failed to manifest the righteousness commanded by God in the Law (Rom 2:12-16). Paul affirms that "the law is holy, and the commandment is holy and just and good" (Rom 7:12). The goal of God's work on our behalf is that "the just requirement of the law might be fulfilled in us, who walk not according to the flesh but according to the Spirit" (Rom 8:4; see also 1 Cor 7:19). In this sense, Jesus is the "end of the law" (Rom 10:4) in the sense that he is the "goal" toward which the whole Law was aiming and the one through whom we have the Spirit that enables an obedient and just life. When Paul argues that Christ-followers "are not under law but under grace" (Rom 6:14), this cannot be interpreted to allow us to continue to be comfortable in our sinful way of life while also claiming to be "saved." The complete testimony of Jesus, Paul, James, and every other New Testament writer leaves us in no doubt: following Christ means living righteously and fulfilling God's commandments.

GOD'S PROVISION FOR RIGHTEOUSNESS: THE SPIRIT

We might well cry out with the first disciples, "Then who can be saved?" (Matt 19:25) if the Torah still essentially reveals the mark that disciples are to attain; if Jesus' teachings are aimed more at removing loopholes and intensifying the ethical vision of the Torah; and if only "the doers of the law will be justified." But we would also hear the same response from Jesus: "For

God all things are possible" (Matt 19:26). Here Paul's carefully developed argument in Romans provides the key. The problem was never in the ethical standards laid out by God in the Law; it was in the human being's incapacity to embody those standards as long as the power of sin was at work in them, perverting the Law's intentions for human community. The standards did not need to be changed—lowered, in effect—to what humans could reasonably live up to. The standards did not need to be abolished, leaving humans sinful and twisted, but uncondemned. Rather, humans had to be lifted up, empowered to embody the righteousness God demands.

This, Paul argues, is precisely what God did by sending Jesus—reconcile sinners and God in his death and resurrection—and by sending the Holy Spirit to enable disciples to do what the Law required but could not empower. The triumphant climax of Romans 1–8 is the announcement that God has sent this Spirit to live within believers, providing them with the inner guidance and power to live righteously before God and with one another (Rom 8:1-17; see also Gal 5:13-25). We move here beyond words on a sacred page to the vital, vibrant experience of God's indwelling Spirit, that "other" within that connects the disciple to God as child to father and provides at last the antidote to the power of sin. Because of the gift of the Spirit, discipleship becomes an offering back to God of one's life, presenting "[our] bodies as a living sacrifice, holy and acceptable to God" (Rom 12:1). This offering takes shape as we live according to what pleases God and our fellow believers (see 2 Cor 5:9-10; Rom 15:1-2) rather than ourselves.

DISCIPLES EMBODY
A FAITH THAT WORKS

Side by side, James and Paul might appear to be involved in a heated argument, each disapproving of the other's "gospel": "a person is justified by works and not by faith alone" (Jas 2:24); "a person is justified by faith apart from works prescribed by the law" (Rom 3:28; see also Gal 2:16). If we compare each writer's use of the example of Abraham (Rom 4:1-25; Jas 2:20-24), this impression is strengthened. This is precisely how the two have been played off against each other in the history of New Testament interpretation, with the result that both have been woefully misunderstood.

The basic problem is that Paul and James are assumed to be addressing the same question, a natural mistake given the similarity of language. But Paul only opposes "faith" to "works" when the question concerns how one becomes a part of God's people. A person becomes heir, is adopted as a child of God, by trusting what God has done in Jesus, *not* by performing those particular works, like circumcision, that formerly separated God's people (the Jews) from others (the Gentiles). James is addressing a different question: what *kind* of faith is genuine? James and Paul both answer this question the same way: Genuine faith results in a transformed life that produces goodness and justice in human relationships (Rom 6:1-4, 12-14; 8:2-4, 12-13).

INVITATION TO DISCIPLESHIP

Jesus confronts his would-be followers with this question: "Why do you call me 'Lord, Lord,' and do not do what I tell you?" (Luke 6:46). The invitation to discipleship is an invitation to take Jesus' instructions as the watchwords for our lives and to bring our ambitions, our thoughts, our speech, and our actions all in line with God's vision for righteousness. It means doing not what we want, but what God wants. This is, no doubt, why the language of ownership and servanthood often comes into play, limiting our freedom and our choices.

The essence of living the transformed life seems to be accepting the fact that our lives no longer belong to us, to do with as we please. The promise of discipleship, however, is that we will discover, in obedience to Jesus and the Spirit, perfect freedom.

Genuine faith results in a transformed life that produces goodness and justice in human relationships.

FOR REFLECTION

• What specific instructions about attitude and behavior do you find difficult? What are some areas that you resist the thought of God asking you to change?

• How would you answer Jesus' question, "Why do you call me 'Lord, Lord,' and do not do what I tell you?"

• What specific instructions about attitude and behavior in this week's Scripture readings do you find difficult to follow?

• What areas in your life do you tend to resist the thought of God asking you to change?

Jesus Calls Us to Minister to a Hostile World

INTRODUCTION

The followers of Jesus, throughout the history of Christianity, have often thought about their role within the world. One constant has remained. Christians have always attempted to discern how to be "salt" and "light" within their surroundings. Discerning how we are to be related to the often-hostile world around us is rarely clear-cut, and we debate with one another about what matters and what does not. A recent bumper-sticker reads, "Live for God; don't sweat the small stuff." Yet, what does it mean to "live for God"? How do we define what "small" means? Aren't there "small" matters about which we must be concerned? What seems like a small matter to the world at large may be a vitally important one for Christians.

What is clear is that we are called to be a people set apart from the world; yet we are also called to be part of this world. The Kingdom as a present reality was embodied in the life and death of Jesus and continues to be embodied in the community of Jesus' followers, the church. But it is also a reality that is only partially manifest. And as Christ's followers, we are called to to be agents of transformation in the world.

DAILY ASSIGNMENTS

While reading this week's Scripture, keep in mind the following questions: (1) What difficulties arise, in each passage, for those participating in the mission of the gospel? (2) What resources are available for those participating in the mission of the gospel?

DAY ONE: Matthew 8–10

Jesus' extensive speech forewarns the disciples about the dangers of his mission. Note the benefits for those participating in God's operation.

DAY TWO: Matthew 11–12

Challenges to Jesus' message came from various sources. Examine Jesus' relationship to his family as described here.

DAY THREE: Acts 1–5

This is the primary record about the development and growth of the early Christian community. Note how the mission becomes more expansive, ethnically and geographically, than in the Gospel of Matthew.

DAY FOUR: First Thessalonians

First Thessalonians is likely Paul's earliest letter to a group of Gentile Christians. Turning from idols was a significant lifestyle change for this group. Observe what differences in behavior and outlook separate these Gentile Christians from their neighbors.

DAY FIVE: First Peter

This "letter" is one of the latest written documents in the New Testament. Observe the emphasis on proper behavior toward the community of fellow believers, as well as toward those outside the community.

DAY SIX: Read the commentary in the participant book.

FOLLOWING JESUS

Following Jesus' first public sermon, the "Sermon on the Mount," which establishes the "ground rules" for discipleship within Matthew's Gospel, Jesus begins his public healing activity. Matthew reports *ten* miracles in this collection, a collection of stories that includes healing stories of women (8:14-15; 9:18-26) and men (9:1-8, 27-31, 32-34), exemplifying a public healing mission that is inclusive of gender, ethnicity, and social class (cf. 8:5-13), even though his own earthly mission was focused on the "house of Israel" (e.g., 10:6; 15:24). Such boundary crossing had social implications then and now. Inclusion of the "other," especially those on the margins of society, was central to Jesus' mission, even the Matthean Jesus. Following the report of these miracles, Matthew presents Jesus' relationship to John over against the ruling political authorities and Jesus' tense relationship with the Jewish religious leaders. These tensions continue throughout other segments of Christianity within the first century.

DIG DEEPER

Compare and contrast the particular elements of Acts 1–5 with Jesus' commission of the disciples in Matthew 10. To what extent does the early church go beyond the parameters of Jesus' commission?

In Acts 1–5, a community of followers of Jesus is formed, following Jesus' ascension. We witness here what was only mentioned in Matthew 10. The disciples offer proclamation (Acts 2; cf. Matt 10:7), heal the sick (Acts 3; 5:15-16; cf. Matt 10:8), and appear before rulers and magistrates (Acts 4–5; cf. Matt 10:17-20). In the story of Acts, the Christian mission is no longer only a mission among the "lost sheep of the house of Israel," as the followers of Jesus speak in a variety of other languages (cf. 2:8-11) by the power of the Holy Spirit, even though the setting is the Jewish Feast of Pentecost. The implications of the "day of Pentecost" (Acts 2) will soon reach beyond Jerusalem, one of the important themes of the Book of Acts (see 1:8).

In First Thessalonians, Paul's earliest letter in the New Testament, we learn about conflict in the capital city of Macedonia, a Roman province. One major distinction of this letter from Acts and Matthew is its shift of focus specifically to Gentile territory and to a people who formerly worshiped idols (cf. 1 Thess 1:9). Paul and his fellow workers proclaimed the "gospel of God" (2:2) among them and did not make demands as "apostles of Christ" could (2:7). Furthermore, as these Gentile believers participated in sharing the good news of God's reign, they, too, "became imitators of the churches of God in Christ Jesus that are in Judea," in "suffer[ing] the same things from your own compatriots as they did from the Jews" (1 Thess 2:14). The opposition against this breakaway sect was apparently severe. Such opposition is minimal today in a North American context where Christian faith is the majority religion. We have to look elsewhere, like to Palestine, Sudan, or Bosnia, to find Christians under persecution because of their minority status. In First Thessalonians, then, we see an "alternative" mission—a mission unlike the one expressed in Matthew and the early part of Acts, so closely tied to Jesus' second commission (Matt 28).

Finally, we hear of a similar situation in a document written at the end of the first century, First Peter. The writer encourages fellow believers to expect suffering for "doing what is right" (3:14), so that in this manner of gentleness, "those who abuse you for your good conduct in Christ may be put to shame" (3:16). A shift occurs, at least within this sector of Christianity, away from an aggressive missionary activity, as advocated in Matthew 10 and exemplified in Acts 1–5. Rather, this group should "be ready to make [a] defense to anyone who demands . . . an accounting for the hope that is in [them]" (3:15).

POLITICAL TENSIONS AND THE SPIRIT'S PRESENCE

In Matthew, after Jesus' lengthy discourse on the mission (Matt 10), the disciples of John the Baptist arrive on the scene to determine if Jesus is a messianic figure (Matt 11:2 ff). The association between Jesus and John *and* the concern of John's disciples are political issues. John has been imprisoned by Herod, and they wonder whether Jesus is the Messiah, an expected political figure who will overthrow foreign rule. The writer reminds readers of John's imprisonment, an event that precipitated the beginning of Jesus' own ministry (cf. 4:12-17). But Jesus' opinion of John is clear and public. Jesus prefers the "messenger" to "those who wear soft robes" and live in "royal palaces" (11:8-10), another anti-imperial charge. Yet, even John is less than the "least in the kingdom," which is probably a statement of the redefined power dynamics in the new "empire" (cf. 18:4). In the new community where God reigns, humility and service—not force—lead to greatness (cf. 20:25-28). The Book of Acts envisions a similar restructuring within the band of Jesus' followers.

In the opening of Acts, the disciples of Jesus pose a question similar to that of the disciples of John the Baptist: "Lord, is this the time when you will restore the kingdom of Israel?" (Acts 1:6). Their question implies a militaristic venture. Yet, the response of the resurrected Jesus shifts the discussion, "It is not for you to know the times . . . but you will receive power when the Holy Spirit has come upon you" (1:7-8). This does not mean, for them or for us, that *witnessing* is apolitical. Rather it is a witness to the presence of God's reign in the world, a reign that involves reconceptions of and challenges to all earthly power structures. In fact, following their release from prison (compare John the Baptist), Peter and John met with fellow believers who recognized the opposition of "kings" and "rulers" to the Messiah (4:25-26, citing Ps 2:1). Moreover, the development of this witness within the early Christian community leads to the development of new communities, as "all who believed were together and had all things in common" (2:44; 4:32), so that "there was not a needy person among them" (4:34). It is not as if, however, *every* person agreed to this policy, as tensions arose over the selling of all property (cf. 5:1-10). Those who opposed the economic strategy for this developing community were, according to this writer, also opposed to the Spirit (cf. 5:9). This situation was not simply about bringing one's goods, but developing a community of like-minded desires. This early Christian sect, in light of all of the forces opposed to their establishment, needed the strength and commitment of all of its members. So they interpreted the unwillingness of Ananias and Sapphira as a direct assault on the work of the Spirit (of unity) among them. According to the writer of Acts, the Spirit's role is often tied directly to the unity of the church (cf. 15:28).

The presence of the Spirit was also a result of the proclamation of the gospel within one of the Pauline missions: the Thessalonian Christian community (1 Thess 1:5-6; cf. 4:8). The initial development of this group of believers included difficulties of suffering as well. Unlike the development of the mission within Jewish communities, in this letter we learn of the spreading of the message among Gentile communities, as folks "turned to God from idols" (1:9). The origins of this Christian community were filled with Paul's own conflict with business leaders and the "magistrates" of the city of Philippi (2:2; cf. Acts 16:20-24). The reception of this gospel message, in turn, brought persecution to the Thessalonian believers who "suffered the same things from [their] own compatriots" as did others (1 Thess 2:14; cf. 3:3). While there is no direct charge about property and possessions as we find in Acts, Paul urges these Christians "to work with your own hands" so that they are not "dependent" on anyone (4:11-12).

By the end of the first century, Christianity is several generations old, but the struggle of living out the faith continues. First Peter, one of the latest written documents in the New Testament, gives us some insight into various Christian communities outside of Rome (i.e., the "Babylon" of 5:13), a city quickly becoming the new center of Christianity. There are only vague allusions to any tension with the surrounding political order (1:6; 4:12, 14), which may be indicative of the writer's own lack of distance from the ruling authorities. Writing unambiguously about these authorities within proximity of them may simply be too risky! In fact, we find quite the opposite: "accept the authority of every human institution, whether of the emperor as supreme, or of governors" (2:13-14). There is, however, a balancing principle in that one should "honor everyone," "fear God," and "honor the emperor" (2:17). It is not as if the emperor should receive treatment dissimilar from any other human being. This theme of accepting human authorities runs throughout First Peter, so that "slaves" should obey even "harsh masters" (2:18-20), "wives" should accept "the authority" of their husbands (3:1-6), husbands should "pay honor" to their wives (3:7), and younger elders should obey older ones (5:5). In a society where honor (and conversely, dishonor or shame) was of great importance to the definition of self-worth, these cultural mores are not surprising.. Despite the challenges such ideas have presented to Christians since the first century, and the need to reconceive them in our own context, the goal of such expectation is still appropriate: the community should "have unity of spirit, sympathy, love for one another, a tender heart, and a humble mind" (3:8; cf. 5:5). The prime example for these characteristics is Christ (2:21; 3:18; 4:13).

The pastoral strategy behind these strange injunctions to submission shows acquiescence to the surrounding culture to dispel prejudice against the group and to silence slander with seemly behavior (cf. 1 Pet 3:16). Even First Peter begins to express a slight move away from the standard hierarchical relationships of society by connecting the fair treatment of the husband's wife as necessary for access to God in prayer. This sentiment, of course, is still a step or two removed from the theological rationale provided for this (less than hierarchical) relationship in Ephesians, beginning with each being "subject to one another out of reverence for Christ" (Eph 5:21).

ACTS OF MERCY
ARE PREFERRED

The discussion in Matthew 12 shifts from political to religious controversy, a "divide" that is generally interrelated in the first century. The chapter opens with two events surrounding the sabbath. Jesus and certain Pharisees do not share the same views of sabbath laws. This would not be unusual since many Jews held different opinions about the interpretation and application of these laws. In addition to the appropriation of scriptural passages to support his activity (12:3-5), Matthew's Jesus also provides a broad theological concept that may explain his activity as well: "I desire mercy and not sacrifice" (12:7). This phrase appears earlier in 9:13 but nowhere else in the Gospel tradition. It does not imply that sacrifice (i.e., at the Temple) has been abolished as unnecessary, since it is a citation from Hosea 6:6 (written during a time of continual sacrifices), but rather that showing "mercy" is a more important activity whenever these two are in tension. "Something greater than the temple is here" (12:6): it is mercy. Jesus' "yoke" is kind. For Jesus, "mercy" means that doing good and acting kindly toward one's fellow human beings is preferable to not acting because of the hindrance of some religious observance. According to Matthew, these particular Pharisees desired to destroy Jesus after these two events (12:14). It will be a while, and with more serious charges, before a legal condemnation of Jesus' activity comes forward.

The real surprise comes in the final passage of the chapter (12:46-50). After completing his debate with the Pharisees and discussion with the crowds, Jesus is informed of the presence of his family. But, in a radical contrast to prevailing first-century cultural values, Jesus refers to his own disciples, and *anyone* who does God's will, as his family and never privileges his blood relatives. Since Matthew does not discuss any reactions to Jesus' decision, we can only imagine the oddity of this proclamation. (Compare this with the teaching of First Peter!) In the face of a hostile world, the extended family of God is present to support all followers of Jesus.

As we might expect, the tensions within Gentile Christian communities were different, but are not addressed extensively in First Thessalonians and First Peter. By the end of the century, however, the Gentile Christian community has begun, according to First Peter, to focus more internally in an attempt to forge a more self-sufficient community. When in contact with other Gentiles, the members are urged to act "honorably" as a form of witness (2:12). But the focus in First Peter is that judgment begins "with the household of God" (4:17). The suffering that ensues should not, however, hinder the believer from doing good (4:19).

INVITATION TO DISCIPLESHIP

The hostility that Jesus encountered is paradigmatic for the experience of the early church and continues to be the experience of many Christians across the globe. To be Christian is to be in service, that is, to be part of the mission of God in the world. To be Christian is to participate in acts of mercy more than acts of sacrifice for the religious establishment. To do good for the sake of another person is more important than carrying out a religious obligation that may interfere with the act of kindness.

> **To be Christian is to participate in acts of mercy more than acts of sacrifice for the religious establishment.**

Consider what resources the early Christians had to persevere not only in faith but also in witness and service, and let's ask ourselves this vital question: what specific actions help us to sense the most encouragement and assistance from the Christian community? This is the question that we should ask ourselves and our communities of faith because we need to remind each other that it is not by our own strength that we carry out any genuine mission. In Matthew and Acts, we are told specifically of the presence of the Spirit who is intimately involved in providing the content (cf. Matt 10:20) and the "power" (*dunamis* in Greek, from which we develop our English word, "dynamite") for the mission to which all Christians have been called. Even the sufferings that inevitably come from such a mission simply mean that the Spirit is present (see 1 Pet 4:14). Also, the presence of the community is a prevailing resource since the days of early Christianity. In Acts, the entire community of disciples was gathered together. Peter and John proclaimed the message as a team and consorted with the assembly when trouble arose. Even the sharing of goods (cf. Acts 2:44-45) was a prime example of the communal nature of this mission. Finally, the presence of "love for one another" is a vital resource for continual perseverance in God's mission in the world. As First Peter declares, "love covers a multitude of sins" (4:8), and from such mutual respect and grace for one another comes the necessary ingredients to support one another in the work of God.

FOR REFLECTION

- What resources does the church today have to help it persevere in faith and service?

- What can Christians do to offer encouragement and assistance to one another in ministering to a hostile world?

- In light of this week's reading, what aspects of Christian discipleship do you embody well? not so well?

Jesus Calls Us to Complex Communities of Faith

SESSION

4

INTRODUCTION

The Christian life calls us into community with others. But therein lie both the *benefits* and the *challenges* of true Christian faith. The body of Christ can certainly lend strength and encouragement and wise support to all the "big events" in our families' lives. Yet, like any other human institution, the church can also bring conflict, strife, and division. How can we all be part of the same congregation when we come from such different experiences in life? That is the challenge of the Christian community. But rather than attempting to avoid our differences, we should see them as critical ingredients to a genuine, honest, "flesh and blood" community attempting to discern its shared purpose in the world with eagerness and sincerity.

DAILY ASSIGNMENTS

While reading the assigned Scriptures this week, keep in mind the following questions: (1) What situations and issues arise within congregations made up of members at various levels of spiritual maturity? (2) What situations arise within ethnically diverse congregations? (3) How should congregations work through the potential tensions of diversity within their midst? (4) What are the advantages of such diversity within local settings?

DAY ONE: Matthew 13–14

Matthew collects many of Jesus' parables into a single chapter. Observe the various images for Jesus' central teaching, the presence of the "reign of God."

DAY TWO: Matthew 15–16

Compare how reactions to Jesus' message and action vary from the Jewish leadership to the disciples, his closest followers. Notice how Jesus ignores cultural boundaries and the reaction this creates among those around him.

DAY THREE: First John

This short letter provides insights into the split of an early Christian congregation. Monitor the difference between "inclusive" and "exclusive" language.

DAY FOUR: Acts 10–15

The story of Gentile inclusion into this "Jewish sect" rapidly changes the make-up of early Christianity. Note especially in Acts 15 how the early church discerns God's will and action (e.g., the use of their *experience* in the mission field, etc.).

DAY FIVE: Galatians

Here is another angle on the question of how persons enter the new community of faith. Pay particular attention to Paul's explanation of his conflict with Peter.

DAY SIX: Read the commentary in the participant book.

A "KINGDOM" COMMUNITY IN THE WORLD

Matthew 13 is often called the parable chapter, because in it Matthew records seven of Jesus' parables. This deliberate strategy of bringing together so many parables in a single narrative section is Matthew's signal that readers should interpret each parable in light of the others. Jesus addresses several themes in these stories, all of which describe some aspect of the reign of God in the world. He deals with how the Kingdom grows (cf. 13:1-23; 13:31-32; 13:33), how the Kingdom community consists of diverse members (cf. 13:24-30, 36-43; 13:47-50), and how the appearance of the Kingdom could be a surprise (cf. 13:44; 13:45-46). For our present discussion, we are interested in this second batch of stories.

Jesus tells two compatible stories about the mixed body of Christ. Both emphasize that "wheat *and* weeds" or "good *and* bad fish" will coexist until the "end of the age." Both stress that separation of these good and bad elements will not occur with the assistance of any human agency. Human involvement in such a discriminatory process will only complicate the divisions within the body, because human biases always interfere in such judgments. Recall Jesus' initial Sermon on the Mount in which he acknowledges the human inability to recognize the "log" in one's own eye while pointing out the "speck" in the eye of the other (cf. Matt 7:1-5). Such misguided judgment must cease within the community of Jesus' followers. In fact, Jesus continues, there are some who have proper confession (i.e., "Lord, Lord") without proper action, which will eventually hinder them from full participation in the heavenly kingdom (cf. 7:21-23). But such arbitration is a divine, not human, activity. And that's a good thing.

The coexistence of both the "good" and the "bad" within the same community of believers appears in one of the early church communities represented in First John. In this Christian community, a division has occurred because of theological differences. In contrast to what Jesus' parables in Matthew seem to say, First John suggests that there are limits on how much ideological tension can peacefully coexist. The writer of First John advocates "discerning the spirits," because, as in this case, denying the *humanity* of Jesus is antithetical to the message that "Jesus Christ has come in the flesh" (cf. 4:1-3). Yet, these two "groups" coexisted for a while, until finally those with differing views about Jesus' humanity left. But notice that they were not kicked out. By choosing to leave on their own, however, they expressed their true selves: "They went out from us, but they did not belong to us; for if they had belonged to us, they would have remained with us. But by going out they made it plain that none of them belongs to us" (2:19). After their departure, the writer senses the need to explain their exodus. But, in the spirit of Jesus' parables, the writer of this letter does not advocate direct *removal* of those influenced by an alternative spirit.

The question the "slaves of the householder" ask in Jesus' parable is a perennial one: "Do you want us to go and gather [the weeds]?" The attention of Jesus' followers often turns to the removal of "the weeds." Yet, our interest and energy should be placed elsewhere. In removing apparent "weeds," in attempts to "discern the spirits" prematurely, we inevitably "uproot the wheat" as well. Damage is done throughout the body of Christ when humans take on responsibilities outside of their purview. Instead, our focus should be more specifically on our mission in the world, "doing the will of God," and not on the specific compatibility of each member with the rest of the body. Many of us would rather exclude those who seem most unlike us. We have so many diverse views on politics, preferences, and pleasures that most of us would favor including only persons who act and think just as we do. This is human nature and desire; but the community of Jesus ought not to be so. Some will depart on their own accord and some explanation should be forthcoming. But no one should be dismissed "until the end of the age." For it is possible, by the grace of God, that Jesus' spirit will so permeate the whole group that even those of us who are "weeds" and "bad fish" may find favor before the end of the age.

> **In removing apparent "weeds," in attempts to "discern the spirits" prematurely, we inevitably "uproot the wheat" as well. Damage is done throughout the body of Christ when humans take on responsibilities outside of their purview.**

DEFILEMENT COMES FROM WITHIN

We witness another type of diversity within the stories of the New Testament as well. In Matthew 15, the Pharisees and the scribes confront Jesus primarily because Jesus' disciples apparently disregard the oral "tradition of the elders" by not washing their hands before they eat. Jesus' reaction radicalizes the notion of defilement: "It is not what goes into the mouth that defiles a person, but it is what comes out of the mouth that defiles" (15:11). According to Jesus, the kind of limits the Pharisees and scribes are so concerned with can only hinder access to God and community.

In an analogous story, Peter has a vision in which he is told by God to eat all manner of food items that were generally considered unclean by Jews. Despite the repetition of the vision (Acts 10:16), Peter was still confused because the revelation challenged his cultural and religious tradition. The control such cultural traditions often have over our minds to block divine thoughts is regrettable but real. But this vision prepared Peter for his contact with Cornelius, a Roman centurion. Finally, in the presence of an assembly, Peter confessed, "God has shown me that I should not call anyone profane or unclean" (10:28).

Not everyone accepted Peter's revelation and testimony about his mission among the Gentiles. In fact, "the church, the apostles and the elders" gathered together in Jerusalem to discuss God's actions in the world, especially among the Gentiles. Keep in mind that, from the Jewish perspective, the greatest ethnic divide in the ancient world was Jew and Gentile; so it is logical that "reasonable" people would have problems with Gentile inclusion into this developing movement with Jewish origins. And they did! Not only did Peter address the church, so did Paul and Barnabas, two other prominent missionaries among Gentiles. In the end, leaders of the church decided, "with the consent of the whole church" (Acts 15:22) and the Holy Spirit (15:28), to accept Gentiles into the movement.

> ## DIG DEEPER
>
> Consider why it is important to give up our distinctiveness (male/female, Jew/Gentile, slave/free) to be the church. Think about how our varied identities can add to the richness of our witness or, at times, take away from our witness.

This same issue of Gentile inclusion into the church directly affected at least one of the Pauline communities as well. Paul's Letter to the Galatians offers his theological reflections on this tension, providing us with insight into Paul's thought process not found in the Acts account. While scholars are uncertain whether Galatians 2 and Acts 15 describe the same historical event, we can be certain that they discuss the same controversial idea—

even if at different historical points and from different historical angles. Should Gentile Christians convert to Judaism in order to become *real* Christians? Paul's response is implied in his question: "Did you receive the Spirit by doing the works of the law or by believing what you heard?" (Gal 3:2). Moving from a discussion of their initial experience to Scripture, Paul links believers to the ancestry of Abraham, who also simply "believed God, and it was reckoned to him as righteousness" (3:6). Gentiles are thus justified by virtue of their faith and become offspring of Abraham and heirs to God's covenantal promises. In Christ, then, "there is no longer Jew or Greek, there is no longer slave or free, there is no longer male and female; for all of you are one in Christ Jesus" (3:28).

HUMAN AND SPIRITUAL ENEMIES

None of us should be deceived. Human *and* not-so-human forces do attempt to sow discord within Christian communities. Herod, for example, opposes both John and Jesus. A later Herod opposes the church and kills one of the apostles, James (Acts 12:2). Sometimes this opposition drove Jesus into the wilderness (cf. Matt 14:13). Yet, fruitful mission can occur in less than attractive areas as well, despite the ill wishes of the "enemy." In Jesus' parable of the wheat and the weeds, an "enemy" attempts to disrupt the growth of the wheat by planting bad roots among them. Likewise, the "antichrist" (only mentioned in First and Second John) is the spirit that causes theological confusion in the Johannine community (cf. 1 John 4:3). We should not expect unhindered operations. In fact, our spiritual antennas ought to rise whenever there are no spiritual obstacles. Perhaps we are not as effective as we might think. Whenever truth speaks to power, whenever actions of righteousness and justice are carried out on behalf of the other, then we should expect to have our "safe-houses" invaded by those who never really "belonged to us."

Truth must speak to power whenever challenges come against followers of Jesus, who break down cultural traditions of racism and sexism. Just as John the Baptist challenged Herod (Matt 14), so also must followers of Jesus be prepared to take on the political forces that wish to manipulate and manufacture communities to maintain the status quo. Sometimes the toughest challenges come from within the movement, so that "Pauls" must confront "Peters" directly (cf. Gal 2:11-14). But the reign of God will not be reined in, because even in deserted places Jesus feeds large groups; even where there are only lame, maimed, and blind, Jesus still provides healing and wholeness and physical nourishment. The alternative communities of Jesus must be prepared to speak truth to power, but they will not be left without spiritual nourishment.

Whenever truth speaks to power, whenever actions of righteousness and justice are carried out on behalf of the other, then we should expect to have our "safe-houses" invaded by those who never really "belonged to us."

INVITATION TO DISCIPLESHIP

Jesus' stories about the nature of the community of his followers are powerfully suggestive. Apparently, communities of Jesus are certain to be made up of groups of all types of people. There may be "good" and "bad" fish, "wheat" and "weeds," and even those with "little faith," upon whom Jesus builds his church. Yet, this diversity—spiritual, theological, racial, economic, and political—receives affirmation in Jesus' teaching and in his mission. Even his reluctance to overstep his own mission, beyond the "lost sheep of the house of Israel," provides an excellent example of how God's reign extends far beyond our planned missions. God just may force us out of our comfortable places precisely to operate in situations in which we cannot depend upon human wisdom or strategy. In such cases, God's wisdom and strategy must operate in order for any good to occur. It is in such moments that the Spirit is present to guide, lead, and direct the words and ways of the followers of Jesus. It doesn't take much on our part, except a willingness to act and a "little faith." With such minimal faith, apparently even huge obstacles to accomplishing the work of God will be removed.

FOR REFLECTION

- What are some of your limitations in terms of developing or partici-pating in diverse communities of faith?

- How might you, with the help of the Spirit, address those limitations?

- What areas of diversity characterize your congregation?

- What benefits do you think those areas of diversity bring to the larger body of Christ?

Jesus Calls Us to Serve One Another

INTRODUCTION

As Christians, we are called to live in community as the body of Christ. And as a community transformed by the love of God, we are to live according to that love. But living in community can be quite challenging. Of course, most issues are minor and we learn to deal with one another's personality quirks or the preferences that stem from such traits. But, what happens when real conflict ensues? How might believers attempt to be faithful to God and to one another during these times of crisis? The New Testament has a lot to say on the matter. We cannot, however, simply transfer the guidance of the first century to the twenty-first century, but neither should we immediately ignore it. If deciphered with attention to their original contexts, the ancient biblical texts may still be utilized to great benefit today.

DAILY ASSIGNMENT

As you read through each passage of Scripture this week, keep in mind the following questions: (1) What issues arise that may cause division or may distract a believing body from its goals? (2) How should members of the body deal with issues of conflict among them?

DAY ONE: Matthew 17–18

This is a time of instruction for the disciples, including how to deal with internal tensions. Relate Jesus' story about a forgiving king and an unforgiving servant to Peter's question about the frequency of forgiveness.

DAY TWO: Matthew 19–20

The instruction continues with an emphasis on the cost of following Jesus and his mission. Note the reaction of diverse characters to Jesus' message.

DAY THREE: 1 Corinthians 8–10

Paul explores how the lives of Gentile Christians have been altered in significant ways. Notice that Paul's defense of his apostleship (Chapter 9) occurs between his discussions of idols. What do you think this means?

DAY FOUR: 1 Corinthians 5; 2 Corinthians 2; Third John; 2 Thessalonians 3

Here are several different scenarios describing how early Christian communities dealt with conflict in their midst. Explore any patterns of discipline found in these chapters.

DAY FIVE: Luke 16; 2 Corinthians 8–9; Acts 5:1-11

These chapters deal with issues surrounding finances and possessions in the early Christian movement. Compare and contrast the various expectations regarding how Christians should view money and possessions in light of each situation.

DAY SIX: Read the commentary in the participant book.

SERVING ONE ANOTHER
IN A SPIRIT OF COMMUNITY

The three predictions of Jesus' forthcoming death and resurrection hover over this entire section in Matthew like dark, heavy clouds before a violent storm (cf. 16:21-23; 17:22-23; 20:17-19). When read within their narrative context, each of these passages portrays a messianic figure whose power will be revealed in his death and resurrection, and *not* in an earthly political struggle for human power over the prevailing governmental insttutions. (This does not mean that Jesus is apolitical, without concerns for life in the larger society. For example, within this section Jesus expresses his concern for paying taxes [cf. 17:24-27].) But even Jesus' closest followers do not immediately grasp how Jesus will overturn traditional messianic expectations. After the first prediction (16:21-23), Peter "rebukes" Jesus, prompting a vehement rebuke from Jesus: "Get behind me, Satan!" It is apparent that Peter's traditional Jewish idea of a militaristic Messiah blinds his ability to grasp Jesus' redefinition of the Coming One.

Corporate takeovers, forced bankruptcies, and imperialistic desires serve as reminders of how the body of Christ ought not to live.

This kind of misunderstanding among the disciples does not improve with further repetition of the predictions. Following the second prediction (cf. 17:22-23), the disciples were distressed to hear of Jesus' death (17:23), but soon thereafter still come to him to ask about "greatness" in the Kingdom (18:1). They still do not perceive that the "greatness" of the Messiah would come only through his "death." Even after the third prediction, the mother of the sons of Zebedee requests positions of authority for her sons (Matt 20:20-21)—a striking, albeit misguided, request from a mother (in Mark 10:35-37, it is the sons who ask). Yet it allows Jesus to elucidate his strategy for leadership: "whoever wishes to be great among you must be your servant" (Matt 20:26), a strategy unlike one followed by the "rulers of the Gentiles" (20:25). In our contemporary context, examples abound of how "Gentiles" rule—corporate takeovers, forced bankruptcies, and imperialistic desires serve as reminders of how the body of Christ ought not to live.

DISCIPLINE IN THE BODY OF CHRIST

Jesus' discussion of "true greatness" (18:1-5) leads naturally into a conversation about maintaining relationships within the body. True followers of Jesus must change and become like children, humbling themselves and ceasing to seek power and advantage over others (18:2-4). Followers of Jesus also practice hospitality and compassion, welcome children and others at the margins of society (18:5; cf. 19:13-15). Finally, Christians care deeply enough for other members of the community to restore "wandering sheep" to the fold (18:10-14), *even if* the offense committed by that member is personal (18:15-20).

Jesus lays out his strategy for handling situations in which persons have offended others. If things cannot be cleared up individually, then "witnesses" should be invited to the conversation (18:16). Inviting others to participate in communal conflicts has a long history in Israelite tradition, although restoration is the primary focus in Jesus' words (cf. Deut 17:6; 19:15). The expression "where two or three are gathered in my name" (Matt 18:20) fuses the human and the divine decision during these disciplinary occasions within the body. In this context, the phrase does not refer to a gathering of believers for worship. Eventually, if the conflict remains unresolved, the entire "church" (*ekklesia* is used only in Matthew) should discuss the matter. This discussion may lead to the dismissal of the offender (e.g., 18:17-20), but the church appropriates this decision only as a last resort after a thorough process. The process itself, with its specific steps, points to a procedure of mercy. There are no rash decisions, even after a serious offense. The offender is never dismissed immediately.

Thus, Peter's question is the perennial one of anyone who has ever been deeply offended: "How often should I forgive?" How often should we seek restoration of the offender? How often should we, acting as "shepherd," seek out the one who has gone astray? Jesus' parable resolves the issue with a theological conclusion: only the one who fully comprehends the forgiveness of God is able to forgive (18:33-35). This is a strategy of merciful discipline.

MERCIFUL DISCIPLINE

Conflict within early Christian communities was not uncommon, as is evident in the need for discipline within the body. Paul's Corinthian correspondence provides us with several examples. In 1 Corinthians 8–10, Paul dealt with a situation in which members were sinning against one another and thereby offending Christ (1 Cor 8:12). In Paul's day, a portion of all meat was sacrificed before it was sold at markets. This was the common cultural practice. So Gentile Christians would have participated in the eating of such meat without much thought. In fact, Paul advocates if an unbeliever invites a believer for a meal then the believer should "eat whatever is set before you without raising any question on the ground of conscience." But, if informed that the main dish of the dinner was offered to idols, Paul's advice differed: "do not eat it out of consideration for the one who informed you," and for the sake of the other's conscience (10:25-28). They must consider how their actions affect the other members of the community. Thus, for the sake of weaker members of the community, they should *not* engage in this practice. For if they cause weaker members to fall away from the community, they sin not only against that member, but also against Christ. The Christian community is a community based not on right knowledge—of church doctrine, polity and Scripture—but primarily based on love, love for and service to the other.

Paul understands that the problem is not that there is any substance to the idea that idols have any real power (cf. 1 Cor 8:4-6). The problem is that not everyone in the body shares this knowledge (8:7). Therefore, such knowledge should not allow believers to abuse the freedom they possess from this awareness (cf. 8:8-13). For Paul, the driving force should not be one's freedom in Christ *but* rather, "to the weak I became weak, so that I might win the weak" (9:22), an idea that Paul clearly finds in his understanding of Christ (cf. 11:1). Peter's question about forgiveness echoes again: "How often should I forgive?" No offense seems greater than the forgiveness every follower of Jesus has experienced.

In 2 Corinthians 2, we read of another situation that forces Paul to respond. Does his basic principle of discipline hold true? Paul was apparently offended by someone in the Corinthian congregation during a previous "painful visit" (cf. 2:1-4). The details of the offense are unclear. What is clear in Paul's present response, however, is that the entire community has been affected and has acted (i.e., punished the offender) accordingly

(2 Cor 2:5-6). Now, Paul's principle kicks in: "reaffirm your love for him" (v. 8); "anyone whom you forgive, I also forgive" (v. 10). Paul's strategy of merciful discipline conforms closely to Jesus' teaching in Matthew's Gospel: "For if you forgive others their trespasses, your heavenly Father will also forgive you; but if you do not forgive others, neither will your Father forgive your trespasses" (6:14-15).

PRIORITIES IN THE BODY OF CHRIST

As we have seen, being a member of the body of Christ requires a radical reordering of one's priorities. No longer should our actions be guided by self-interest, but rather by love of our brothers and sisters. This new paradigm of love has implications not only for how we treat one another, but also for how we view things like wealth and possessions and social status. To follow Jesus, as one rich man discovers, requires an alternative perspective about the value and use of one's possessions (Matt 19:16-23). Even Jesus' closest companions view Jesus' challenge to potential followers who are wealthy as too radical (19:25). Again, Peter asks the difficult question about what will be gained once all is left behind to follow Jesus. Jesus' response is twofold. On the one hand, there is much to gain (19:28-29). Those who follow Jesus will inherit eternal life. On the other hand, Jesus tells a parable (unique to Matthew) enclosed by the dominant principle of the section, the "first will be last, and the last will be first" (19:30; 20:16).

> **Being a member of the body of Christ requires a radical reordering of one's priorities. No longer should our actions be guided by self-interest, but rather by love of our brothers and sisters.**

The parable of the laborers in the vineyard (Matt 20:1-16) challenges conventional notions of fair wages. Jesus tells a story that would have been a common experience in the surrounding culture, as laborers gathered at the market daily seeking work. In this story, the landowner is not viewed as unfair, since he fulfills his agreements with laborers. Nonetheless, it seems reasonable that the person who labored all day should receive *more than* the one who worked only for one hour. But that is the twist in the story. The point is not about how much work has been accomplished or how many possessions have been accumulated (cf. 19:16-22). This is not laissez-faire economics. Such additional labor does not invite any distinctive divine blessing. Each of the laborers fulfilled his agreed-upon obligations. Yet the landowner chooses to be more generous to those who have worked less (cf. 20:15). In the end, the wages were equally distributed so that each family could have enough food for the day. In some ways, an egalitarian model is presented here (except, of course, for the landowner himself). A growing number of scholars suggest that this parable summons followers of Jesus to welcome a more egalitarian worldview—economically and socially—as an essential component of the reign of God on earth.

In Luke, Jesus tells a related story about the appropriation of another person's wealth (16:19-31). In this instance, the rich man failed to provide any kindness for poor Lazarus who lay at his gate. He did not "sell and give." The rich man dies and departs to Hades. His eternal destiny is intimately associated with his failure to deal with common needs surrounding his house. In a similar story, in the later Christian community, others laid only a percentage of their goods at the feet of the apostles (Acts 4:34–5:6). Like the rich man, Ananias and Sapphira also die, although quite unnaturally. Once again, as in Matthew 19–20, the emphasis in Acts 5 is on the sharing of goods so that "it was distributed to each as any had need" (Acts 4:35). Renewing one's mind in relationship to the appropriation of one's possession is a central theme throughout the biblical story.

DIG DEEPER

To what extent did the fair distribution of goods continue as a common practice among the early church? Do some research to explore the economic values and practices that characterized Christianity beyond the New Testament period.

Was fair distribution of goods the common practice in the early development of the church? It seems so. But why? We can turn to some of Paul's reflections in Second Corinthians for a theological rationale for this strategy. As Paul urges the church "to excel also in this generous undertaking" of raising funds for the poor saints in Jerusalem, he explains his rationale as looking for a "fair balance" rather than a burden on those who give (2 Cor 8:13-15). Finances should not hinder followers of Jesus from seeing the needs of others. Rather, with the grace of Christ as the chief exemplar, it is quite appropriate for believers to use their finances in ways that show this commitment to the one who "was rich, yet for your sakes he became poor, so that by his poverty you might become rich" (2 Cor 8:9).

INVITATION TO DISCIPLESHIP

If Jesus' life of service and dedication to the other, even to the point of death ("giving himself as a ransom"), is the point of departure for a life of discipleship, then the concerns of the other should be a higher priority for the body of Christ. Such a strategy seems foreign in an individualistic society like our own, where what I think, how I act, what I choose is most important. But, followers of Jesus should beware. The one who follows Jesus must consider the other as a child who should not be hindered from entering the Kingdom, as a sheep who should be returned to the fold, as an offender who should be forgiven over and over again, and as a poor saint for whom the sharing of goods is essential. When grace and power are interwoven to secure meaningful relationships with others, this fusion becomes a sign of God's powerful grace and self-giving power on behalf of all.

One clear example of this reconceptualized perspective is the manner in which Jesus' followers should view and appropriate their financial means. Throughout the New Testament, it is striking that the wealthy are constantly challenged to envision a world in which their possessions belong to God and not solely to themselves. This is already a challenging idea. Why are the wealthy not forgiven "seventy-seven times" for their offense to others, perhaps due to a misappropriation of their funds? This is a question that is often asked by those of us who live and benefit from the wealth of our own nation. Can our wealth really hinder a committed relationship with God? If so, how so? The New Testament imagines a world where no one goes hungry and where those of us who have much participate in caring for the "poor saints" as part of our larger mission in God's new world order, after the model of the one who came "not to be served but to serve, and to give his life a ransom for many" (Matt 20:28).

FOR REFLECTION

- When have you experienced grace beyond expectation from another human being?

- When have you encountered a fellow believer as a sheep to be returned to the fold or as an offender to be forgiven? How did you respond?

- When have your possessions, or the pursuit of them, been a hindrance to your relationship to God?

Jesus Calls Us to a New Relationship with Tradition

INTRODUCTION

Commitment to one another includes the negotiation of our lives in the context of a pledge to be in community. Oftentimes, this cooperation, to give and to receive, is worked out in a community that has a history before any newcomers arrive. In those contexts, there are clear (although often unstated) "traditions" about what to do and when to do it and what not to do. Some groups are more lenient about which rules may be broken and the length of the grace period they may allow for "amateurs" to get up to speed. Some of these traditions are fundamental to how these communities define themselves, so ignoring them is no small matter. The best communities of faith consciously, and in good conscience, assess and reassess these commitments to tradition or else the community itself loses its vitality.

DAILY ASSIGNMENTS

As you read through each passage of Scripture this week, keep in mind the following questions: (1) What kinds of religious traditions exist within the body of Christ? (2) Are there any that hinder us from being the body of Christ? (3) What are some ways to negotiate our way through the "traditions of the faith" without simply jettisoning them?

DAY ONE: Matthew 21; 1 Peter 2:4-10; 1 Corinthians 3:16-23; 6:12-20; John 2:13-22

Each of these passages provides insight into early Christian redefinition of the Temple in light of the coming of Jesus. Note the function of the Temple for early Christians.

DAY TWO: Matthew 22

The Pharisees and Sadducees, religious leaders concerned with protecting the Jewish religious tradition, drill Jesus on matters of religious and social practice. Pay attention to their specific reactions. Recall Jesus' declaration in 5:17 that he comes to fulfill, not abolish the law. How does Jesus transform these "traditions" rather than simply break them?

DAY THREE: Matthew 23

Jesus condemns the actions, not the words, of the Pharisees. What does Jesus suggest about the limits of tradition?

DAY FOUR: Romans 9–11

Paul grapples with the benefits and the limits of the tradition of his ancestors. Note the positive features of these traditions for the Jews.

DAY FIVE: Hebrews 7; 11

The writer of Hebrews also struggles with the benefits and the limits of the Jewish tradition. Think through how the writer of Hebrews defines faith, particularly in a context in which tradition is critical for understanding relationship with God. (Notice how the writer uses examples of people from the history of Israel to illustrate faithfulness.)

DAY SIX: Read the commentary in the participant book.

THE ROLE OF TRADITION

From its inception, the church has had to struggle with the traditions—the practices, beliefs, and sacred text—it has inherited and how to make those traditions relevant, living, and vibrant for each generation. Few traditions are kept wholeheartedly; few are rejected unequivocally. The remaining traditions are revised within and reconfigured for present-day communities to make them relevant and meaningful. Part of this negotiation is because "tradition" (lit. a "handing over" or "transfer," from the Latin *traditio*) is really a "conversation" between our Christian forebears and us. As Paul writes, "I handed on to you as of first importance what I in turn had received" (1 Cor 15:3; cf. Matt 28:8-10; John 20:14-18). Tradition often provides the lens through which we read the scriptural texts, playing a significant part in the interpretive process between readers and texts. Or, to say that differently, interpretation involves a constant and dynamic interplay between Scripture, tradition, the Holy Spirit, and our own reason and experience. None of them (i.e., readers, Scripture, or tradition) leaves the discussion without being changed and affected by the others.

Jesus, too, negotiated with the tradition in which he had been raised and that had provided meaning, sustenance, and survival for the people of God. As we discussed in Session 2, the Sermon on the Mount provided the Matthean basis for Jesus' mission. This mission often involved a way of carrying out the tradition as provided in the community's understanding of the Torah: "You have heard that it was said to those of ancient times." The tradition provided the field in which he worked. Yet this field was not an area of confinement, but a place to learn where to go within the boundaries. For example, "you shall not murder" sets up, for Jesus, a trajectory that "you should not even be angry" with a fellow believer. Or, "you shall love your neighbor and hate your enemy" sets up a trajectory that "love for the enemy" is the more apt response. Sometimes Jesus' teachings flowed naturally from the tradition; sometimes they did not. This, however, was the function of tradition for the Matthean Jesus. As Jesus stipulated for "every scribe" at the end of the parable chapter (Matt 13), training to be one of his followers involves "[bringing] out of [one's] treasure what is new and what is old" (13:52).

IMAGES OF THE TEMPLE
IN EARLY CHRISTIANITY

Jesus' cleansing of the Temple is one of the most confrontational acts in the Gospel tradition. With this event, Jesus directly, even if only symbolically, challenges the practices surrounding the central symbol of his own religious heritage. The Jewish priests responsible for its maintenance could not sit by idly and thus confronted Jesus as he was teaching in the Temple (cf. 21:23-27). Most scholars think that this confrontation, prompted by Jesus' actions, is the primary reason for the charges against Jesus that led to his death (cf. Mark 11:18; Luke 19:47).

For Matthew, Jesus' authority to cleanse the Temple is legitimated by his prophetic status (cf. Matt 21:11, 46). Jesus' citations from Isaiah and Jeremiah (21:13) establish this link further: " 'My house shall be called a house of prayer'; but you are making it a den of robbers." Jesus offers a prophetic critique of the economic practices of this institution but does *not* attempt to stop all practices associated with sacrifices at the Temple. Yet, his actions at the "center" of Judaism opened up an opportunity, for ill or for good, for the early followers of Jesus to begin to reconceptualize a religious worldview in which the Temple was not at the center of understanding the presence of

> ### DIG DEEPER
>
> Learn more about the Temple in the time of Jesus, to put into perspective his critique of the central symbol of faith. Look for images of how the Temple looked both before and after its destruction in A.D. 70.

God in their midst. The historical destruction of the Jerusalem Temple in A.D. 70 gave impetus to imagining a world without the Temple, but such reflection on this tradition had already begun.

Paul's letters to the Corinthians, written a decade and a half before the destruction of the Jerusalem Temple, imagines the "body" (of Christ) or gathered community as the "temple" in which the Spirit of God dwells: "Do you not know that you are God's temple and that God's Spirit dwells in you?" (1 Cor 3:16). Again, in 1 Corinthians 6:19, Paul refers to the body as the temple: "Or do you not know that your body is a temple of the Holy Spirit within you, which you have from God, and that you are not your own?" It may be difficult to grasp the communal nature of this message in English translations. But the *you* in this verse is plural, as is the possessive *your* in 6:19. The Spirit of God dwells within the body of Christ, or among the members of the body of Christ. An individualistic notion that each member is an individual temple of God in which the Spirit dwells is *not* what Paul means. For Paul, there is an intimate relationship among the community of believers, and it is this relationship that constitutes the "temple" in which the Spirit dwells.

Other Christians in the early church also attempted to rethink the tradition of the Temple and its function and implications for the new movement. In John's Gospel, the story about Jesus' action in the Temple concludes with the association of his own "body" as the new Temple (cf. John 2:19-21). In language similar to Paul, First Peter encourages Christians to accept the rebuilding of themselves "into a spiritual house, to be a holy priesthood, to offer spiritual sacrifices acceptable to God through Jesus Christ" (1 Pet 2:5). In the Book of Revelation, there is "no temple in the city" because the Temple is now equated with the presence of "the Lord God the Almighty and the Lamb" (Rev 21:22), the latter part of which connects suitably with the Johannine tradition.

All of this shows a dynamic, vibrant enterprise in which many Jews, including the followers of Jesus, were engaged in the hard theological work of trying to reconsider the function of the tradition surrounding the Temple, as the particular place of God's special presence. They sought to reinterpret the tradition in light of their new experience and belief that God's presence has now come uniquely in the arrival, mission, death, and resurrection of Jesus of Nazareth.

THE ROLE OF THE LAW SINCE CHRIST HAS COME

Did such reconceptions cause a clear divide with their Jewish forebears? Paul addresses this concern directly in the Letter to the Romans. It is not surprising that he would discuss the matter in this "essay" because the community to whom he writes is an ethnically mixed body, with diverse traditions. In the latter part of the document, Paul addresses conflicts regarding eating kosher food (14:2) and observing of special days (14:5-6), which are examples of tension that existed between the observant Jewish believers and nonobservant Gentile believers. Paul tackles the issue of eating practices and encourages each member "never to put a stumbling block or hindrance in the way of another" (14:13).

Yet, Paul spends thoughtful effort attempting to explain how these traditions have been fulfilled with the coming of Christ. As for the law, for example, Christ's arrival is the "end" (*telos* probably means "goal," as in purpose, rather than "end," as in termination) of the law (10:4). Right relationship with God is now completely determined by relationship with Christ (10:3). That God has established Christ as the "stumbling stone" over which many Jews have stumbled is one key idea that Paul shares with the writers of First Peter and the Gospel of Matthew (Rom 9:33; cf. 1 Pet 2:6-8; Matt 21:42).

For Paul, as important as these traditions are, God has chosen a "remnant" (Rom 11:5), of which Paul himself is a part (11:1). Yet, even this remnant does not exhaust the mysterious ways of a graceful God (e.g., 11:12, 15, 25-29). The story of how God has dealt with the people of Israel will have implications for their future destiny, despite how the various relevant traditions are conceived.

> **The story of how God has dealt with the people of Israel will have implications for their future destiny, despite how the various relevant traditions are conceived.**

For another reconsideration of the tradition of the law, the writer of Hebrews provides an alternative suggestion, which seems to go one step beyond Paul. It is not that the law was abrogated, but that the type of priesthood such a law demanded was no longer necessary in light of the appearance of Christ, a priest in the order of Melchizedek: "For when there is a change in the priesthood, there is necessarily a change in the law as well" (Heb 7:12). The law proves ineffective because it is tied closely to the levitical priesthood, an earthly, mortal lineage (7:23). But Christ is a heavenly, eternal priest who makes continual intercession on behalf of his followers (7:24). This new type of priest makes relative the role of the law in the life of the new community.

JUSTICE, MERCY, FAITH, AND TRADITION

In Webster's dictionary, the term *Pharisee* is defined briefly in this manner: "a hypocrite; a self-righteous person." Similarly, the Random House College Dictionary says, "a sanctimonious, self-righteous, or hypocritical person." The editors of these American dictionaries may well have been reading Matthew 23, in which Jesus forcefully challenges these tradition bearers. But all of what Jesus says in this chapter should be read in light of the opening few verses: "Do whatever they teach you and follow it" (23:3). All of it should be read in light of Jesus' words in the earlier sermon, "unless your righteousness exceeds that of the scribes and the Pharisees, you will never enter" (5:20). It seems unreasonable to suggest, in light of Jesus' comparison, that the Pharisees were not a serious, and highly influential, religious movement during the first century. Jesus' "woes" against the tradition's bearers is not a direct attack on tradition itself, but an attack on its appropriation especially when "justice, and mercy, and faith" are disregarded (23:23). Religious practices ought not to replace genuine acts of piety for the sake of others. For this Jesus states clearly, "I desire mercy and not sacrifice" (9:13; 12:7).

Religious practices ought not to replace genuine acts of piety for the sake of others. For this Jesus states clearly, "I desire mercy and not sacrifice."

INVITATION TO DISCIPLESHIP

The struggle with tradition is essential to faithful living in Christ. Crucial to that enterprise is an ongoing dynamic discussion with our forebears (i.e., the tradition), with the scriptural story of God, and with others theologically different from ourselves. We find precedent for all of these discussions within the sacred texts themselves and, thereby, find the freedom to engage advisedly and forthrightly in these vibrant conversations that are all around us. We proceed advisedly because our goal is to become more faithful followers of the one who encourages us to know the Scriptures *and* the power of God (cf. Matt 22:29) for living out the mission of justice and mercy in God's creation. We proceed forthrightly because our honesty about the traditions that hinder us, and God's work among us, is critical for all who desire to follow the only instructor among us, the Christ (cf. 23:12).

None of these New Testament passages suggest that we should disregard the tradition outright without thoughtful reflection. Tradition itself represents a story about the way those in the past have experienced and expressed the work of God among them *and* can often function as a historical corrective to our contemporary situation. For this reason, tradition should be honored and not ignored. At the same time we must also continually decide the extent to which that tradition still rings true for us.

FOR REFLECTION

- In Matthew 23:23, Jesus criticizes the Pharisees for having "neglected the weightier matters of the law: justice and mercy and faith." To what extent do you neglect these matters?

- What traditions (e.g., biblical teachings, church doctrines, congregational practices) seem to hinder faithful living today?

- What traditions seem to be a corrective to faithful living today?

Jesus Calls Us to Live in Light of His Coming Again

INTRODUCTION

How often have you thought, usually with more than a hint of regret, "if only I had known how things would turn out, I would have done something different"? Perhaps you made a bad investment of time or money. Perhaps you put too much of yourself into a relationship that went bad. Perhaps you unexpectedly lost a loved one without clearing up some misunderstanding. Jesus invites us to live in the here and now so that we will *not* experience that pang of regret, magnified a thousandfold, when we stand before him at the threshold between this life and the life of the world to come.

DAILY ASSIGNMENTS

As you read this week's assignments, take note of how discussions of the "end" function to relativize the claims being made by the political and ideological voices of the first century. Pay attention also to how the disciples are challenged to live in light of their "insider's knowledge" of God's plan to intervene in human history. How does this knowledge free us for more authentic living?

DAY ONE: Matthew 24–25; Luke 21

Jesus predicts his disciples will face difficulties before his coming again. Of special importance are the ways this knowledge should affect how they live in the interim period. What guidance do you find in these texts regarding how disciples should live in the present?

DAY TWO: 1 Thessalonians 4:13–5:11; Hebrews 10:19-39; 2 Peter 3

Three different apostolic voices underscore the relationship between their convictions about what God will do in the future and how to engage present challenges. How does the promise of Christ's return sustain the early Christians during their suffering?

DAY THREE: Revelation 1–3

John places the situation of his seven congregations squarely between Jesus' presence in their midst now and Jesus' coming in glory to judge at "the end." What does Jesus commend about how each of the churches is living out their faith? What does he censure as behavior that jeopardizes their future in him?

DAY FOUR: Revelation 4–7

John looks beyond the impressive displays of emperor-worship and Roman power to cosmic scenes of worship, commissioning, judgment, and redemption. Pay attention to how John's vision places God and Christ at the center of all things, to what responses are due this creating God and redeeming Lamb, and to the results of living or not living with God at the center of one's life.

DAY FIVE: Revelation 17–19; 22

John shows his readers what Roman imperialism "looks like" in light of God's vision for human community. Observe what practices and effects of Rome's political domination John finds objectionable and why.

DAY SIX: Read the commentary in the participant book.

DON'T BE FOOLED
BY APPEARANCES

Jesus would have made a terrible tour guide. Tour guides are trained to heighten the "oo!" and "ah!" experience of visitors to a city or attraction. When his disciples expressed awe at the grandeur of the Temple in Jerusalem, Jesus threw a wet blanket on their enthusiasm. The Temple was meant to look impressive. Herod the Great had undertaken a major renovation project to make the Temple a wonder of the ancient world. The huge stones that so impressed the disciples conveyed a sense of inviolability, stability, even eternity. The Temple was central in the life of the Jewish people, a symbol of God's presence with God's people and, therefore, of the impregnability of Jerusalem: "God is in the midst of the city; it shall not be moved" (Ps 46:5).

The visible appearance of the Temple had its desired effect in the eyes of the disciples, but Jesus could not allow his friends to be taken in by the solid appearances of the present. He knew where things were heading, and that in a not-too-distant tomorrow the Temple would lie in smoldering ruins. The leaders of Jerusalem would violently suppress Jesus and his disciples, and God would bring destruction upon the unrepentant city: "See, your house is left to you, desolate" (Matt 23:34-39). This is certainly how Luke, writing after the destruction of Jerusalem at the close of the first Jewish Revolt of A.D. 66–70, understood Jesus' words in retrospect.

Therefore, Jesus had to prepare the disciples to give up the symbolic center of their world. Their sense of security and their sense of connectedness with God could not be allowed to remain bound up with the Temple that had structured the life of Israel for centuries. Jesus knew that their message would bring them into bitter conflict with the defenders of the status quo, a conflict that began in earnest shortly after the Resurrection and soon claimed lives (recall the stories from Acts 4; 5; 7:2–8:3; 9:1-2). He therefore prepared them for the alienation they would face from the structures that had formerly given their lives meaning: "they will hand you over to be tortured and will put you to death" (Matt 24:9; see also Luke 21:12-19). He also sought to protect his followers from getting caught up in the agendas and lies of competing revolutionary factions that would arise between his resurrection and the destruction of the Temple in A.D. 70. Jesus cautioned them to remain detached from any nationalistic-religious program so that they could remain faithful to God's agenda for their lives and their mission: "False messiahs and false prophets will appear and produce great signs and omens" (Matt 24:24; see also Matt 24:5-8, 11, 23-26; Luke 21:8-11). In other words, by revealing to them what would happen in the future, he freed them from becoming ensnared by the priorities of those who lived only for the present and from being left confounded after building their lives and sense of security around deceptively "solid" structures.

UNVEILING THE PRETENSIONS OF EMPIRE

The belief that Jesus would return and usher in a kingdom that would indeed outlast time had clear ramifications beyond Jerusalem as well. When Paul writes to the Christians in Thessalonica, a Roman colony that was particularly proud of its deep-rooted association with Rome and her emperors, he takes a thinly veiled shot at the ideology of Roman rule. Rome justified her domination of the Mediterranean with her claims of bringing "peace and security" (1 Thess 5:3). *Pax* ("peace") and *securitas* ("security, stability") were common slogans of empire, appearing on the reverses of many coins or in proclamations about the benefits of the emperor's rule. They were believed to be the cards that trumped allegations concerning the underside of empire—the oppressive burdens of taxation and compulsory service, the siphoning off of the best products of the provinces, and the violent suppression of any resistance or potentially subversive elements.

DIG DEEPER

Explore the realities of living in the Roman Empire of Paul's day, using a Bible dictionary or similar resource. Consider why Rome's claims of *pax* and *securitas* would have been threatened by Paul's proclamation of the gospel.

Paul, however, holds the highest trump card. Both those who promoted the ideology of Roman rule and those who allowed themselves to be lulled into believing that peace and security were to be found in the strength of Rome were destined for disappointment. Rome would not last: "When they say, 'There is peace and security,' then sudden destruction will come upon them" (1 Thess 5:3). All its illusions about itself were about to be shattered by the coming King who would return to deliver those who lived by his Spirit, directing their steps by God's marching orders. Consider the way non-Christians encounter death, grieving "as others do who have no hope" (1 Thess 4:13-14). None of Rome's promises mean anything in the face of death, the final reality. But those who build their lives around their relationship with God, while grieving the loss of loved ones, would also find hope and strength in their assurance of God's future. Living by the priorities of being found "ready" when Jesus returns rather than building one's life around the promises of Rome can be compared to sobriety rather than drunkenness, or walking in a well-lit path rather than stumbling around in the darkness (1 Thess 5:5-8).

No book examines everyday realities in the light of God's sovereignty and Christ's coming so powerfully and pervasively as does The Revelation to John. Readers in the modern period have especially mistaken its form, namely an endless stream of predictions, with its function. Revelation rigorously examines the writer's and audiences' contemporary situation in the light of the broader unseen realities in God's realm—the realm of demonic activity, the past history of the cosmic conflict that plays itself out on the human stage, and the resolution of that conflict. The Book of Revelation is an *apocalypse*, one of a large family of texts that pay attention to sketching out the "larger canvas" of time and space. The book is aimed to give readers the "big picture," ultimately revealing the significance of the visible realities that dominate their everyday world. Apocalyptic language is often written from the margins—not necessarily by the poor and persecuted, but at least by those who consider themselves in some way "on the outside." Apocalypses give such marginalized people the rhetorical power they need to topple the dominant ideology and its hold over their readers.

The first readers of Revelation in Asia Minor would have had no difficulty recognizing in the beast of Revelation 13 their self-glorifying emperor, worshiped as a god throughout the province. They would also have readily seen the harlot of Revelation 17 and 18 as an exposé of the goddess Roma, the personification of the city that ruled the known world from its roost upon seven hills (17:9, 18). John immerses himself and his readers in the voices of the Hebrew prophets, internalizing their witness to God's vision for human community and their trenchant critique of the ways domination systems pervert and hinder God's vision by weaving webs of political oppression and economic exploitation. By showing his readers what Roman imperialism "looks like" in the light of God's judgment and Christ's kingship, he liberates their minds from the lies of imperial propaganda. This "freedom," however, carries with it the obligation to witness boldly to God's vision for human community through visible withdrawal from sick and exploitative systems and creation of a community of justice and holiness in the churches.

WHAT SORT OF PERSONS SHOULD WE BE?

In all their various descriptions of the "end time," the New Testament writers shared at least one conviction: that the priorities, investments, and ambitions of followers of Christ should all be shaped by the knowledge of that end. Popular writers today have invested themselves too heavily in trying to hammer all these "predictions" together into a coherent "map" of the end. In so doing, they have distracted our attention from the way each New Testament writer would shape our faithful response to God by the awareness that, in the end, only God and what belongs to God will survive.

Being "ready" recurs throughout apocalyptic literature as a constant refrain. The four parables that crown the apocalyptic discourse in Matthew 24–25 thrust "being ready" to the forefront of every disciple's agenda. Paul and John both stress the dangers of being found unprepared, of not living as people who look ahead to Jesus' coming in glory and judgment (1 Thess 5:3-4; Rev 1:7). "Watching" for Jesus' return is nothing other than applying ourselves fully to the work of extending love and mercy to which Jesus appointed us (Matt 24:45-51; 25:31-46). It means being prepared for the "delay" so that we do not slacken in our discipleship and get caught unprepared in the end like the bridesmaids with no oil in their lamps (Matt 25:1-13). It means using the resources that the Lord entrusts to us to bear the kind of fruit that pleases him (Matt 25:14-30, 31-46). The end-time language reorders our everyday priorities in light of eternal realities.

> **In all their various descriptions of the "end time," the New Testament writers shared at least one conviction: that the priorities, investments, and ambitions of followers of Christ should all be shaped by the knowledge of that end.**

"Since all these things" that seem so solid and valuable to worldly minded people "are to be dissolved in this way," we are invited to invest ourselves in the cultivation of Christ-like hearts, the fruit of the Spirit, and in one another (2 Pet 3:11-12, 14), rather than investing ourselves in the affairs of a world order that is destined to come to nothing.

The Letter to the Hebrews and the Book of Revelation both bear witness to how our hope for Christ's return, and our conviction that the judgments that the world passes on believers are of limited value, can embolden disciples to keep following God's call even in the face of opposition (see Heb 10:32-39; Rev 2:2-3, 9-10, 13). Because disciples live in the light of eternity, they can take the "long view" of things and not get caught up in the propaganda and pursuits that sustain domination systems. Indeed, they are invited to live as witnesses to a different kind of world order—one in which people are redeemed for God, are endowed with dignity, and work to ensure the good of all rather than secure the abundance of the few at the cost of the many.

But Jesus always surprises us. In Revelation, the "Coming One" surprises us by showing up already in our midst (Rev 1:12-13, 20; 2:1-2, 16, 22) or by standing at our thresholds (Rev 3:20). He is already present to see, to weigh, to reward, and to judge. John invites the disciples in first-century Asia Minor to make some very specific decisions about how they will respond to the hostility of neighbors, the social and economic pressure to engage in idolatry, the lure of wealth purchased through cooperation with imperialism, and the cost of discipleship. John asks them to evaluate their actions not only in light of Christ's future coming in judgment upon Babylon (Rev 19:1-21), but also in light of Jesus' scrutiny of their allegiances, motives, and works in the present (Rev 2:1–3:22).

INVITATION TO DISCIPLESHIP

The apocalyptic literature of the New Testament is ultimately about establishing priority. For two thousand years, these texts have proclaimed to Christians that "in a very little while, the [Coming One] will come and will not delay" (Heb 10:37). For two thousand years, the Coming One has, in fact, delayed. This is a problem that even the New Testament writers wrestled with.

The writer of Second Peter confronts the real problem of the delay and, frankly, disappointment head-on by asking his readers first to consider time from God's eternal perspective and, second, to interpret the delay as a sign of God's patience toward those who still had not repented and returned to God.

Jesus' invitation to live now in the assurance that he will come again does not demand of us that we neglect these historical facts. Rather, it demands we continue to proclaim to ourselves and to our world that we are all accountable to a God who is above our political, economic, and personal agendas; who has revealed God's agenda for humankind; and who will indeed hold us accountable for what we do and what we fail to do. The promise of Jesus' return frees us from the lie that our jobs, our goods, our power, our relationships—even our country—provide the stable center for our lives and invites us to find in God, and in the active doing of God's will, the secure ground upon which to build our lives. The imminence of the end in the New Testament always serves the pastoral purpose of helping us prioritize our faithful response to God and investment of ourselves in what pleases God. Whether Christ comes to us or we go to him, he remains the final reality in our lives; therefore "making it our aim to please Him" remains the first priority of disciples (2 Cor 5:9-10).

FOR REFLECTION

• In what areas of your life are you showing, and doing, what most pleases God?

• What areas of your life show that your primary sense of stability comes from things that are temporary?

• How do this week's readings challenge you to review and revise your priorities?

Jesus Calls Us to Experience the Gifts of His Dying and Rising

SESSION

8

INTRODUCTION

The central focus of Christian belief has always been the cross and resurrection of Jesus Christ. Paul reflects this when he recites what is perhaps the earliest Christian creed, which he faithfully received and handed on: "that Christ died for our sins in accordance with the scriptures, and that he was buried, and that he was raised on the third day in accordance with the scriptures" (1 Cor 15:3-4). The New Testament writers explore how such a death could in fact be "for us" and its significance "for us" and our relationship with God. They also teach consistently that the love, godly obedience, and humility Jesus showed in dying "for us" provides a model for our own lives together (in relationships of mutual commitment to this ideal, not in abusive relationships), as well as the path to eternal life.

DAILY ASSIGNMENTS

As you read through this week's Scriptures, keep in mind the following questions: (1) What is the writer contributing to the early church's interpretation of, and quest for meaning in, the death and resurrection of Jesus? (2) How is the writer connecting Jesus' experience of death on the cross and his resurrection with our experience as Christian disciples?

DAY ONE: Matthew 26–28; Psalm 22

The reading from Matthew narrates the last days of Jesus' earthly ministry—and the inauguration of his eternal ministry. Pay close attention to Jesus' attitude as he approaches his death and to the clues Matthew provides to the meaning of his death.

DAY TWO: Hebrews 8:1–10:18; Leviticus 16

The writer of Hebrews presents a rich interpretation of the significance of Jesus' death and ascension using the ritual imagery of a final and complete "Day of Atonement." How does Jesus' death and entry in heaven change God's perception of us and our perception of ourselves before God? How does it change the way we are able to encounter God?

DAY THREE: Romans 5–6; 8

We have already read parts of Romans 5–8 in connection with the theme of the transformed life into which Jesus calls his followers. This time, look closely at how Paul interprets the death and resurrection of Jesus. Also, observe the direct connections he makes between Jesus' experience of death and resurrection and the new life that opens up for us as his disciples.

DAY FOUR: Philippians 2–3; 1 Peter 1–2; 4

Today's readings especially draw out the implications of Jesus' suffering and death for the disciples who follow in his way. Pay attention to the guidance about how Jesus' cross takes shape in the attitudes, actions, and experiences of disciples, both in their interactions with other disciples and with nonbelievers.

DAY FIVE: 1 Corinthians 15; 2 Corinthians 4–5

Paul is convinced that the resurrection of Jesus, which is the promise of our resurrection, completely changes our orientation to life in this body. In what ways do you see Paul's faith in the Resurrection enabling a more completely cruciform life?

DAY SIX: Read the commentary in the participant book.

THE HORROR OF THE CROSS

The Gospel story has a strange climax. The man who taught with authority, who cast out demons with power, who restored sinners, and who healed the afflicted with compassion and love—but who also boldly challenged the Temple authorities on their own ground—is nailed to a Roman cross to die a criminal. Film versions of this story can erase from our minds the polished and clean images of gilt crosses and crucifixes and present the bare and brutal reality of capital punishment in the backwaters of the Roman Empire. Indeed, making sense of the very reality of this brutal and degrading execution of their leader was the primary obstacle to the Christian message early Christians had to overcome: the writer of Hebrews speaks of Jesus enduring a cross, "disregarding its shame" (Heb 12:2); Paul speaks of Jesus humbling himself to the point of enduring not just "death" but "*even* a death on a cross" (Phil 2:8, emphasis added); and Paul again speaks of preaching a crucified man as a deliverer as "foolishness" and "offensive" to Greeks and Jews (as in 1 Corinthians 1:23).

THE MEANING OF THE CROSS AS A DEATH "FOR US"

Like most other writers of New Testament texts, Matthew gives careful attention to spelling out how Jesus' death was a meaningful one. Jesus' crucifixion by the Roman and Jewish leaders did not simply represent the elimination of a dangerous rival, although Matthew certainly gives due weight to the very human, political factors contributing to Jesus' execution throughout his Gospel (Matt 21:45-46; 26:3-4; 27:1-2, 18). Rather, it was a death that Jesus embraced "for many" (Matt 20:28), "for us" (Rom 5:8), "for you" (1 Pet 2:21).

The typical crucifixion scene involved Roman soldiers dragging off resisting criminals to the place of execution and pinning them down long enough to nail them to the cross and hoist them aloft. Matthew says Jesus' death was very different. Despite appearances, it was not a life "taken"; it was a life "given" (Matt 20:28; 26:26-28). One way that Matthew brings out the voluntary nature of Jesus' death is through Jesus' predictions of his passion, death, and resurrection (Matt 16:21-23; 17:22-23; 20:17-19; see also 17:12; 21:38-39; 26:2, 11). Jesus saw it coming and went ahead willingly and purposefully. The scene of Jesus in Gethsemane shows the difficulty of the decision to go forward, but also again the voluntary nature of his death as he keeps his instincts to flee in check. Throughout Jesus' arrest and trial, Matthew preserves the sense of a life "given" in Jesus' command to his followers not to resist (26:52), in his declaration of his ability to summon legions of angels to deliver him (26:53), and in his refusal to defend himself from the accusations at his trial (26:63; 27:14). In different language, John also emphasizes Jesus' "gift" of his life: "The good shepherd lays down his life for the sheep. . . . No one takes it from me, but I lay it down of my own accord" (John 10:11, 18).

Matthew also points away from the agenda of Jesus' rivals and political authorities to the will of God as the ultimate force behind his crucifixion. Matthew repeatedly affirms that Jesus' death occurs as the fulfillment, in some sense, of "the scriptures" (Matt 26:24, 54, 56), a general claim echoed by many New Testament writers (as in 1 Pet 1:10-12 and 1 Cor 15:3-4; see also Luke 24:25-27, 44-49). Matthew also makes this claim implicitly by portraying Jesus' crucifixion in ways that directly recall Psalm 22, suggesting that the psalm was being fulfilled there on Golgotha. (The Psalms were treated as prophetic oracles both by early Christians and by the members of the Qumran sect.)

In so doing, Matthew joins the ranks of many New Testament writers who connect Jesus' death and resurrection with the Hebrew Scriptures both in terms of the details of its narrative and its meaning. We see examples of the latter in 1 Peter 2:21-25, which illumines Jesus' death through the lens of Isaiah 53, and in Hebrews 8–10, which interprets his death through the lenses of the prophecy of the "new covenant" in Jeremiah 31 (quoted in Heb 8:7-12) and the Day of Atonement ritual in Leviticus 16.

DIG DEEPER

Compare Matthew 27:32-50, (especially verses 35, 39, 43, 46) with Psalm 22. How does the story of Jesus' death in Matthew echo details from the Psalm? Think about how Matthew's readers, familiar with Psalm 22, would have reacted to that connection.

Jesus' death, "foretold" or "announced" in Scripture, thus becomes a feature of God's plan for bringing deliverance to God's people and demonstrates God's movement behind the scenes of history to orchestrate and bring about this death on a cross. Jesus' crucifixion becomes a revelation of God's love for humanity and God's provision for an alienated people planned long ago but sent "at the right time" (Romans 5:6-11; 8:31-32, 38-39). Jesus' self-giving is the outworking here of God's self-giving and God's faithful commitment, not to abandon his creatures, but to bring them back to himself.

But how is this death "for us"? How does it change our circumstances? Earlier in his Gospel, Matthew calls Jesus' death a "ransom for many" (Matt 20:28). The image of "ransom" connects with the social experience of slaves or prisoners of war having to be "bought back" from the state of slavery or from the enemy. In the readings from Session 7, John the seer also uses the language of ransom or redemption, speaking of Jesus "buying back for God" a people brought together from every tribe, language, people, and nation (Rev 1:5-6 and 5:9-10). These people are bought back from sin, a superhuman force that "owned" humanity prior to Jesus' death (Rom 8:2-4, 10-11). They are bought back from "the futile ways inherited from [their] ancestors" (1 Pet 1:18-19), a way of life that addicted them to idolatry, self-gratification, and the quest for precedence over other people (1 Pet 4:1-6). They are "set free" from slavery to the fear of death (Heb 2:14-15), so that they are no longer afraid to give away their own lives for the sake of God's cause in the world, knowing God's resurrection power as well. They are "set ... free from the present evil age" (Gal 1:4), no longer bound by the rules of human domination systems—and no longer destined to die with them.

The images of ransom and redemption through shed blood also suggested to early Christians that Jesus' death was a kind of sacrificial rite performed "for us." The Passover, in which the blood of a lamb redeemed the firstborn children of Israel, provided the closest parallel; but New Testament writers quickly identified the sin offerings and the Day of Atonement sacrifices as an important background to understanding the meaning of Jesus' death. Matthew hints at this as early as 1:21, when the angel names the child *Jesus* because "he will save his people from their sins." Matthew explicitly links Jesus' death to an offering for sin in 26:28 (contrast Mark 14:24), where Jesus calls his blood the "blood of the covenant," the shedding of which brings "forgiveness of sins" (see also 1 Cor 15:3; 1 Pet 2:21-25). Matthew uses a phrase familiar from Exodus 24:8, where Moses pours out "the blood of the covenant" at the altar to signify that the Torah is now binding upon the Hebrews. Now, however, the shedding of Jesus' blood brings the "new covenant" of Jeremiah 31:31-34 into effect, the result of which is forgiveness of sins.

Paul also finds sacrificial language helpful to express the meaningfulness of Jesus' death (as in Rom 3:21-26). Jesus was "put forward as a sacrifice of atonement by his blood" (3:25). This death is given to God as an act of obedience that reverses the effects of Adam's original act of disobedience now infecting the entire human race (Rom 5:12-21), making many righteous (5:19) and reconciling us with God (5:1-11).

But it is the writer of Hebrews who provides the most detailed and thorough interpretation of Jesus' death as a sacrifice for our sins. In Hebrews 8–10, he uses the background of the covenant inauguration sacrifice of Exodus 24:3-8 *and* the Day of Atonement ritual of Leviticus 16 as central for understanding the significance of Jesus' death and ascension into heaven. The new covenant announced in Jeremiah 31:31-34 promised to plant God's desires for our lives within us, on our hearts, and to "forgive and forget" all our sins against God. Jesus' death was the sacrifice that inaugurated this new covenant (Heb 9:15-22, recalling Exodus 24:3-8). On the Day of Atonement, the Levitical high priest offered several animal sacrifices to remove sin from the people and to cleanse the Holy of Holies, the innermost room of the Temple, of the invisible yet dangerous defilement caused by that sin. Thus he repaired the relationship of a sinful people with the Holy God. These rituals were ultimately ineffective, however, since the people could never be so thoroughly cleansed as to enter into God's presence in the Holy Place themselves. Jesus performs the final and complete "Day of Atonement" ritual, sanctifying the people (Heb 9:11-14; 13:12-14) and going, not into the earthly Temple, but into the heavenly Holy of Holies to remove the defilements caused by the sin of the people (9:23-28). Jesus offers his "body" as the perfection of the animal sacrifices that God rejected (the distinctive interpretation of Ps 40:6-8 in Heb 10:1-18). By so doing, Jesus opened wide the way into "heaven itself," preparing us to live forever in the very presence of God.

FOLLOWING A CRUCIFIED MASTER

Jesus' death and resurrection, however, is not just a series of acts performed for our benefit; it is an invitation to follow. Matthew defined discipleship as cross-bearing, which meant serving others as Jesus served rather than serving ourselves and finding true life by giving away our lives as Jesus did (16:24-28; 20:25-28). Paul thought this absolutely essential. For him, there was no sharing in the resurrection of Jesus without first sharing in the cross of Jesus. We are to conform our minds, hearts, and lives to the character of Christ, shown in his obedience to the point of death on a cross (Phil 3:8-11). Writing to his friends in Philippi, Paul defined cross-bearing in very practical terms: "Do nothing from selfish ambition or conceit, but in humility regard others as better than yourselves. Let each of you look not to your own interests, but to the interests of others" (Phil 2:3-4). Such self-emptying is the necessary remedy for those of us who are too full of ourselves. It is important, however, that self-emptying be offered voluntarily and out of the fullness that we have in God, and not as the response of a submissive member in an abusive relationship or system.

Cross-bearing also means dying to sin, to that way of life and to those particular activities that draw us away from holiness and justice. Paul holds up baptism as a significant teaching tool for disciples on this point (Romans 6:1-14). The gift of baptism is that we are joined to Christ in his death, so that we are freed from the power of sin, and rise with Christ to "walk in newness of life." Remembering our baptism can help us remember who we are—no longer the "old person" that our sinful desires and our society's preoccupations crafted us to be, but the "new person" that the Spirit is bringing to life within us. Cross-bearing means showing courage when confronted with the hostility of others who are still trapped in their own "old persons" and refusing to give away God's gifts of new life for the sake of appeasing them (as in 1 Pet 2:18-25; 4:12-16).

Remember, however, that the cross is not viewed apart from the Resurrection in the New Testament. Jesus' resurrection proclaims "cross-bearing" to be God's approved way to live. It is the hope of resurrection that puts life in *this* body in perspective and enables faithful discipleship when obedience becomes costly. When life in this body is compared with the Resurrection body, a shift in values and emphasis takes place (as in 1 Cor 15:42-44; 2 Cor 4:7-5:17). Those who follow a crucified Messiah no longer seek out that which makes them "look" impressive or enhances "appearances." Rather, they look for and value those experiences of God's transforming power at work in their lives and the lives of others, changing hearts and forging Christ's character within them. This transformation leads them to the outward expression of this Christ-like character, even if that means that the "appearances" suffer (2 Cor 4:7-12, 16-18). Ultimately, we have no power in our bodies to survive death, no matter how "impressive" we make ourselves. Jesus' cross and resurrection give us freedom from that pervasive obsession and enable us to follow God's leading and the life of the Spirit, knowing that God alone gives life to the dead.

INVITATION TO DISCIPLESHIP

"If any want to become my followers, let them deny themselves and take up their cross and follow me" (Matt 16:24). Discipleship as understood by Matthew, Paul, Peter, or the writer of Hebrews means cross-shaped living.

The cross-staff was a navigational tool used during the thirteenth through sixteenth centuries. It was constructed simply of a long stick with a shorter horizontal crossbeam that could slide up and down the longer stick. Religious poets quickly perceived the metaphorical potential of this instrument. Just as a ship's pilot calculated his position and charted his course by taking measurements of sun and stars with the cross-staff—lining up his reality with the cross, as it were—so the Christian disciple navigates his or her way. Through each encounter, each decision, each opportunity, a follower of Jesus measures his or her response by the humility, the self-giving love, the obedience to God, the commitment to serve the other, and the fortitude displayed by Jesus as he took up the cross for us by his own choice. All genuine Christian discipleship is thus marked with the sign of the cross.

Yet the cross is never the be-all and end-all of Christian discipleship. Just as Jesus' cross led to God's exaltation of the resurrected Jesus to God's right hand, and just as the cross-staff as a navigational tool was useful only to lead its users to their appointed destination, so cross-shaped living is hope-filled living. It looks forward to sharing with Christ in the eternal rewards that God has prepared for those who choose to live by God's ways rather than the world's ways. The cross-shaped life bears consistent witness to worldly minded people that their grasping for power, their preoccupation with appearances, and their gratification of their self-serving desires are misguided efforts to secure short-lived goods. It calls us to bear witness to God's model of leadership—redemptive, self-giving, other-serving—to the powers of this world who oppose the cross. It remains an invitation to others to experience the freedom from those dead-end obsessions that following Jesus brings, a freedom that enables us to live beyond death by giving away our lives in imitation of the Lord "who gave himself for our sins to set us free" (Gal 1:4).

FOR REFLECTION

• In your current situation, where do you see yourself walking most in line with Jesus' example?

• Where in your faith are you challenged by what the cross represents?

• How does Jesus' dying and rising change the way you see yourself before God?

VIDEO ART CREDITS

OPENING SEQUENCE

Sermon on the Mount by Kim Hak Soo © Asian Christian Art Association

Christ Washing the Disciples' Feet by Adrian Kupman / SuperStock

Christ Before Caiaphas by Gerrit van Honthorst / Museo Civico, Prato, Italy / Bridgeman Art Library

Crucifixion (Christ of San Placido) by Diego Rodriguez Velázquez. Museo del Prado, Madrid, Spain. Scala / Art Resource, NY

Last Judgment, ceiling fresco. Abbey of the Augustinian Canons, Vorau, Austria. Photo by Erich Lessing / Art Resource, NY

ART PANELS

Detail of Christ's Head. Stations of the Cross War Memorial, Dublin. Photo by Graeme Outerbridge / SuperStock

Nativity (2001) by He Qi © He Qi. Used by permission of the artist

Sermon on the Mount by Kim Hak Soo © Asian Christian Art Association

The Calling of Saints Peter and Andrew, early Christian mosaic. S. Apollinare Nuovo, Ravenna, Italy. Scala / Art Resource, NY

Pentecost by Jesus Mafa © Jesus Mafa

The Sower by Jean Francois Millet © Burstein Collection / CORBIS

The Red Vineyard at Arles, 1888 by Vincent Van Gogh. Pushkin Museum of Fine Arts, Moscow, Russia. Scala / Art Resource, NY

Jesus Welcomes the Children by Kim Jae Im © Asian Christian Art Association

Christ Driving the Traders From the Temple by El Greco. National Gallery, London / SuperStock

Last Judgment, ceiling fresco. Abbey of the Augustinian Canons, Vorau, Austria. Photo by Erich Lessing / Art Resource, NY

Crucifixion (Christ of San Placido) by Diego Rodriguez Velázquez. Museo del Prado, Madrid, Spain. Scala / Art Resource, NY

TEXTILE ART

Banners by: Sandra Briney Designs
512 East Broadway Avenue
Medford, Wisconsin 54451
www.sbweavingdesigns.com

VIDEO CREDITS

Segment 1, Part 1

Codex Syrus Sinaiticus. Used by permission of the Holy Council; St. Catherine's Monastery; James Charlesworth; Princeton Theological Seminary and Bruce Zuckerman; West Semitic Research Project / Biblical Archaeological Society

Jesus by Daniel Nevins / SuperStock

Segment 2, Part 1

Sermon on the Mount by Kim Hak Soo © Asian Christian Art Association

Moses and the Ten Commandments by James Jacques Tissot / The Jewish Museum, NY / Art Resource, NY

Segment 3, Part 1

Priene, Turkey. Record of Paulus Fabius Maximus, Roman governor of Asia, proposing to the Asian League of cities that they change their calendar so that Augustus's birthday would be henceforth New Year's Day. Uses the term "Gospel" (*euangelion*) for Augustus. Bildarchiv Preussischer Kulturbesitz / Art Resource, NY

Emperor Augustus in Military Dress / Vatican Museums, Vatican State / Photo by Erich Lessing / Art Resource, NY

Life of Christ, detail with six scenes from the New Testament. Mosaic. Baptistry, Florence, Italy. Scala / Art Resource, NY

Segment 4, Part 1

Abraham and the Three Angels by He Qi © He Qi. Used by permission of the artist

Segment 5, Part 1

First Isaiah Scroll / Photo by John Trevers / Biblical Archaeological Society

Christ Before Caiaphas by Gerrit van Honthorst / Museo Civico, Prato, Italy / Bridgeman Art Library

Christ Washing the Disciples' Feet by Adrian Kupman / SuperStock

Segment 6, Part 1

Qumran Settlement, Aerial View / Photo by Werner Braun / Biblical Archaeological Society

Mosiac of the Apse Right Side: *Melchisedec.* Church of Sant' Apollinare in Classe, Ravenna, Italy. Canali Photobank, Milan / SuperStock

Segment 7, Part 1

Psalter of Ingeburg of Denmark, The Last Judgement, Resurrection of the Dead. Musée Condé, Chantilly, France. Giraudon / Art Resource, NY

The Beast Rising from the Sea by Giusto de Menabuoi. Baptistry, Padua, Italy. Alinari / Art Resource, NY

Segment 8, Part 1

Resurrection of the Dead by Paul Chenavard. Église Parochiale, Bohal, France. Photo by Erich Lessing / Art Resource, NY

The Empty Tomb by Jesus Mafa © Jesus Mafa

NOTES

NOTES

Praise for

KIKI INSIDE THE SHADOW CITY
STRIKE

A *Teenreads* Best Book of the Year
A *Washington Post* Best Book of the Year
A *San Francisco Chronicle* Best Book of the Year

"If Harry Potter lived in New York City, he'd have a mad crush on 14-year-old Kiki Strike . . . the next literary idol of the tween-to-infinity set. Kiki's creator, Kirsten Miller, is destined to become the object of millions of readers' adoration." —*Vanity Fair*

"I loved this book, and so did my 11-year-old daughter—and we're rarely on the same page about anything. . . . A terrific and completely original read. **A**" —Tina Jordan, *Entertainment Weekly* (online)

"Non-stop thrills starting from page one challenge the reader to put it down while the mysteries deepen, leaving the curious begging for answers." —Teenreads.com

★ "A fascinating, convoluted mystery-adventure, which features early-adolescent girls with talents and abilities far beyond their years." —*Booklist*, starred review

"This is a rallying cry for the 'curious' and an effective anthem of geek-girl power. . . . An absurdly satisfying romp." —*Kirkus Reviews*

"Miller pulls readers in immediately and takes them on a series of twists and turns, culminating in a thrilling climax. . . . *Kiki Strike* celebrates the courage and daring of seemingly ordinary girls." —*SLJ*

"An edge of your seat thriller that is both brilliantly original and also whip smart." —Bookslut.com

"[A] deliciously entertaining debut novel. . . . The author's love for New York's nooks and crannies shines from every page, making this a rare adventure story." —*Publishers Weekly*

"A thoroughly entertaining, not-to-be-missed story for anyone hungry for adventure and mystery." —*The San Diego Union-Tribune*

"Perfect for bright middle-schoolers hooked on history and mystery." —*The Washington Post Book World*

"The theme of empowerment through brains and bravery is carried through seamlessly, and the plot thrums with the thrill of discovery. . . . I am privileged to introduce all of you to these new (and soon to be iconic) female characters in young adult fiction—the indomitable, spirited Kiki Strike and her friends." —*The MetroWest Daily News*

"Author Miller has created an exciting (and definitely sequel-scented) spy adventure with clever, resourceful heroines." —*St. Paul Pioneer Press*